THE PASS

Life stories that converge, entangle, entwine, and enchain. How lucky when your own crosses paths with exceptional people. People who give everything at every moment, freely and without complaint. People with the gift to turn your daily routine into a thing of wonder.

They share their lust for life, their art of living, with you. They make you strong. For all that, I thank them for being there.

I thank a father, a grandfather, a beautiful individual who gave everything to his little guy, his "meccutt." Thank you for helping him to this day to become in turn . . . a good person.

K, Espé's wife

writing & illustrations   ESPÉ

colors   Aretha BATTISTUTTA

THE PASS

Some stories are invented, others are told. . .

graphic mundi

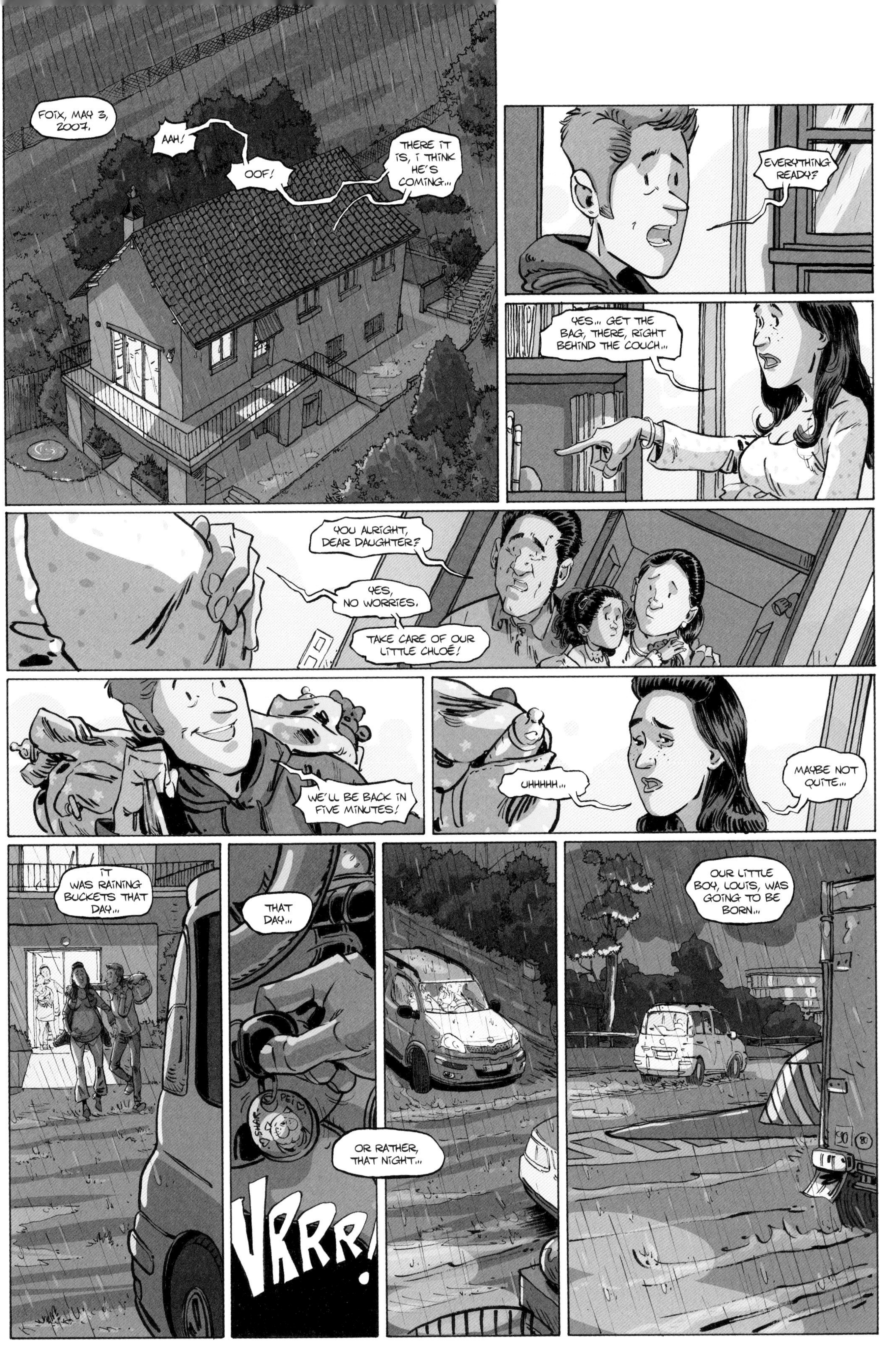
FOIX, MAY 3, 2007.
AAH!
OOF!
THERE IT IS, I THINK HE'S COMING...
EVERYTHING READY?
YES... GET THE BAG, THERE, RIGHT BEHIND THE COUCH...
YOU ALRIGHT, DEAR DAUGHTER?
YES, NO WORRIES.
TAKE CARE OF OUR LITTLE CHLOÉ!
WE'LL BE BACK IN FIVE MINUTES!
UHHHHH...
MAYBE NOT QUITE...
IT WAS RAINING BUCKETS THAT DAY...
THAT DAY...
VRRR!
OR RATHER, THAT NIGHT...
OUR LITTLE BOY, LOUIS, WAS GOING TO BE BORN...

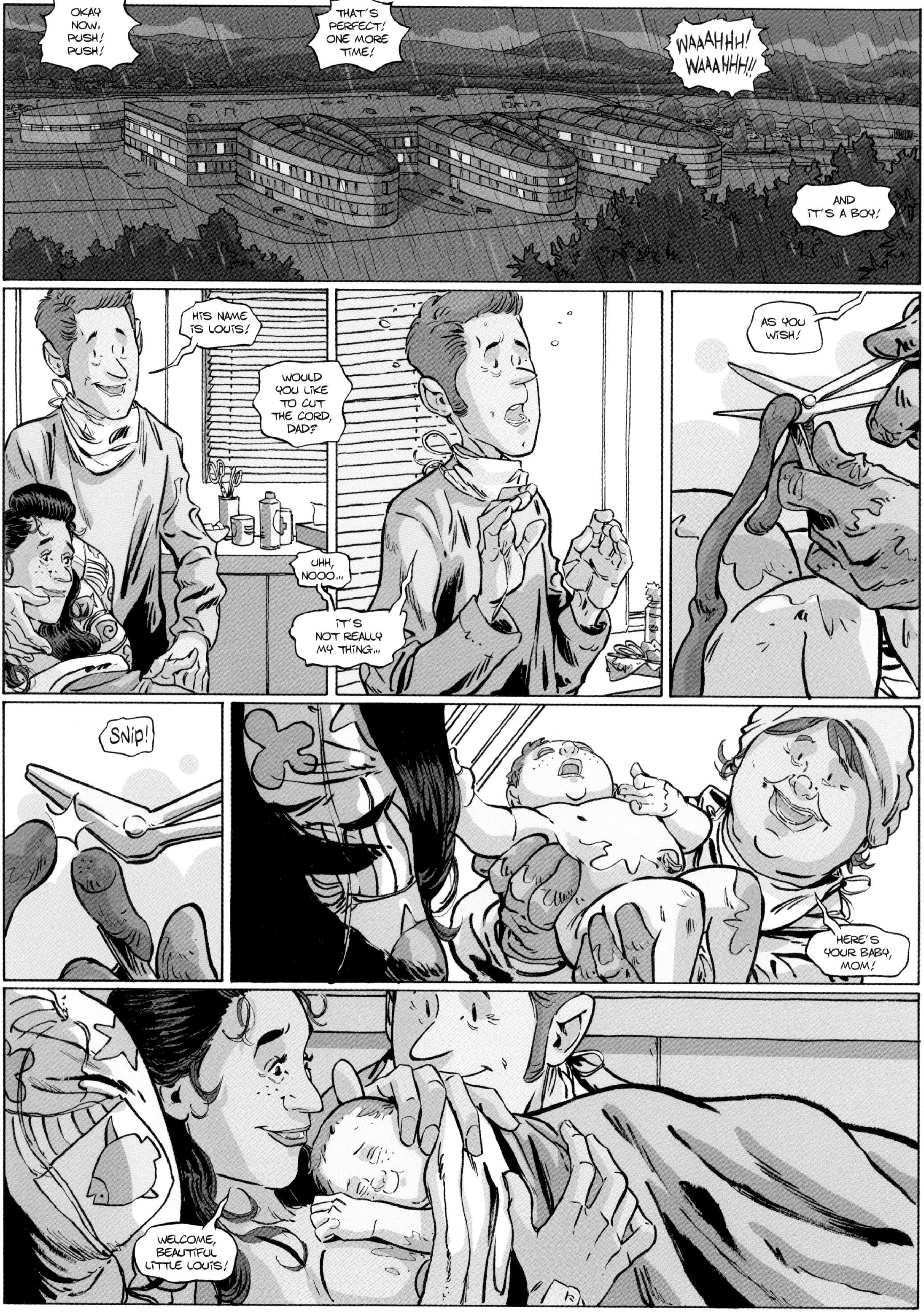
OKAY NOW. PUSH! PUSH!
THAT'S PERFECT! ONE MORE TIME!
WAAAHHH! WAAAHHH!!
AND IT'S A BOY!
HIS NAME IS LOUIS!
WOULD YOU LIKE TO CUT THE CORD, DAD?
UHH, NOOO...
IT'S NOT REALLY MY THING...
AS YOU WISH!
SNIP!
HERE'S YOUR BABY, MOM!
WELCOME, BEAUTIFUL LITTLE LOUIS!

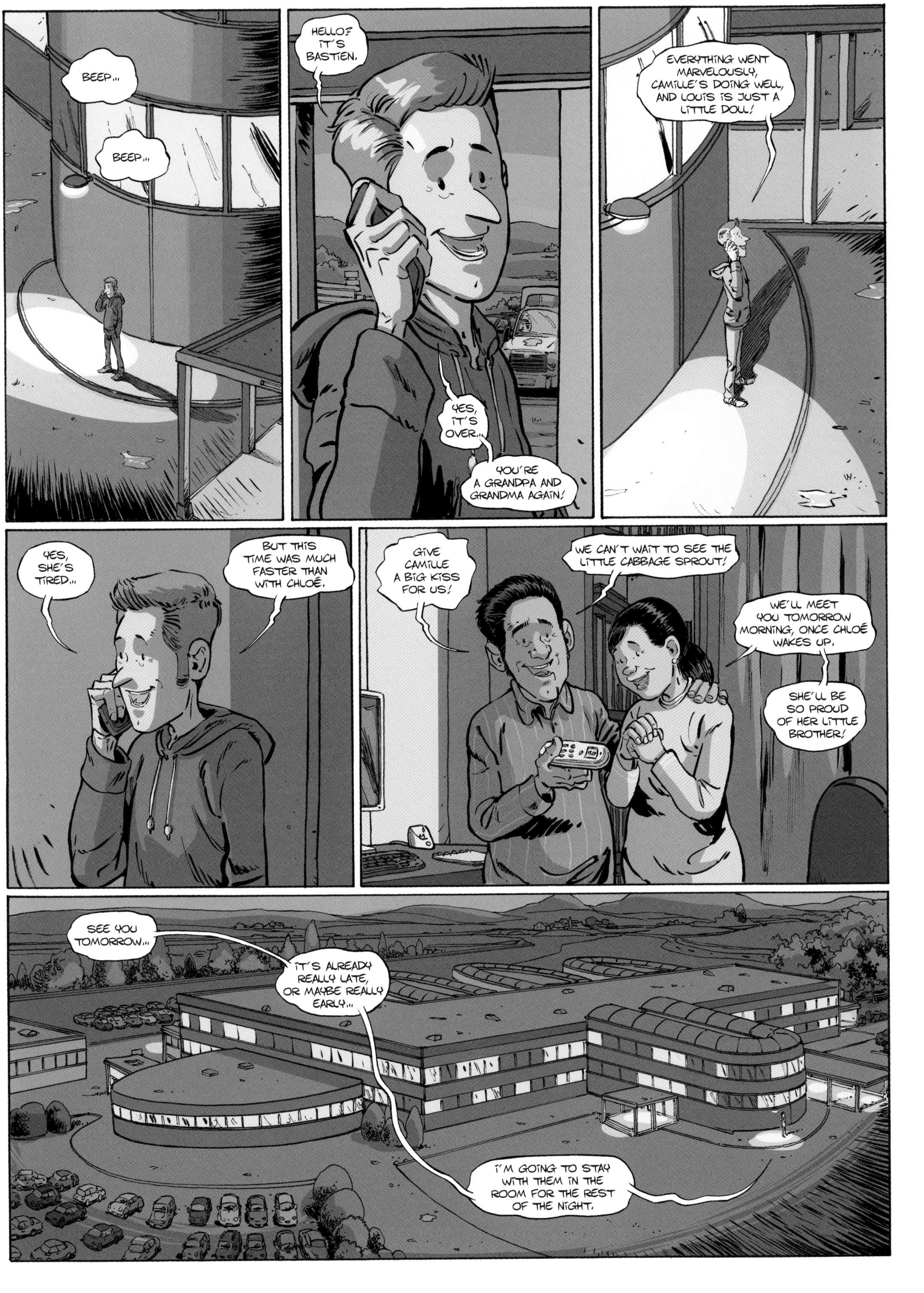
BEEP...
BEEP...
HELLO? IT'S BASTIEN.
YES, IT'S OVER...
YOU'RE A GRANDPA AND GRANDMA AGAIN!
EVERYTHING WENT MARVELOUSLY, CAMILLE'S DOING WELL, AND LOUIS IS JUST A LITTLE DOLL!
YES, SHE'S TIRED...
BUT THIS TIME WAS MUCH FASTER THAN WITH CHLOÉ.
GIVE CAMILLE A BIG KISS FOR US!
WE CAN'T WAIT TO SEE THE LITTLE CABBAGE SPROUT!
WE'LL MEET YOU TOMORROW MORNING, ONCE CHLOÉ WAKES UP.
SHE'LL BE SO PROUD OF HER LITTLE BROTHER!
SEE YOU TOMORROW...
IT'S ALREADY REALLY LATE, OR MAYBE REALLY EARLY...
I'M GOING TO STAY WITH THEM IN THE ROOM FOR THE REST OF THE NIGHT.

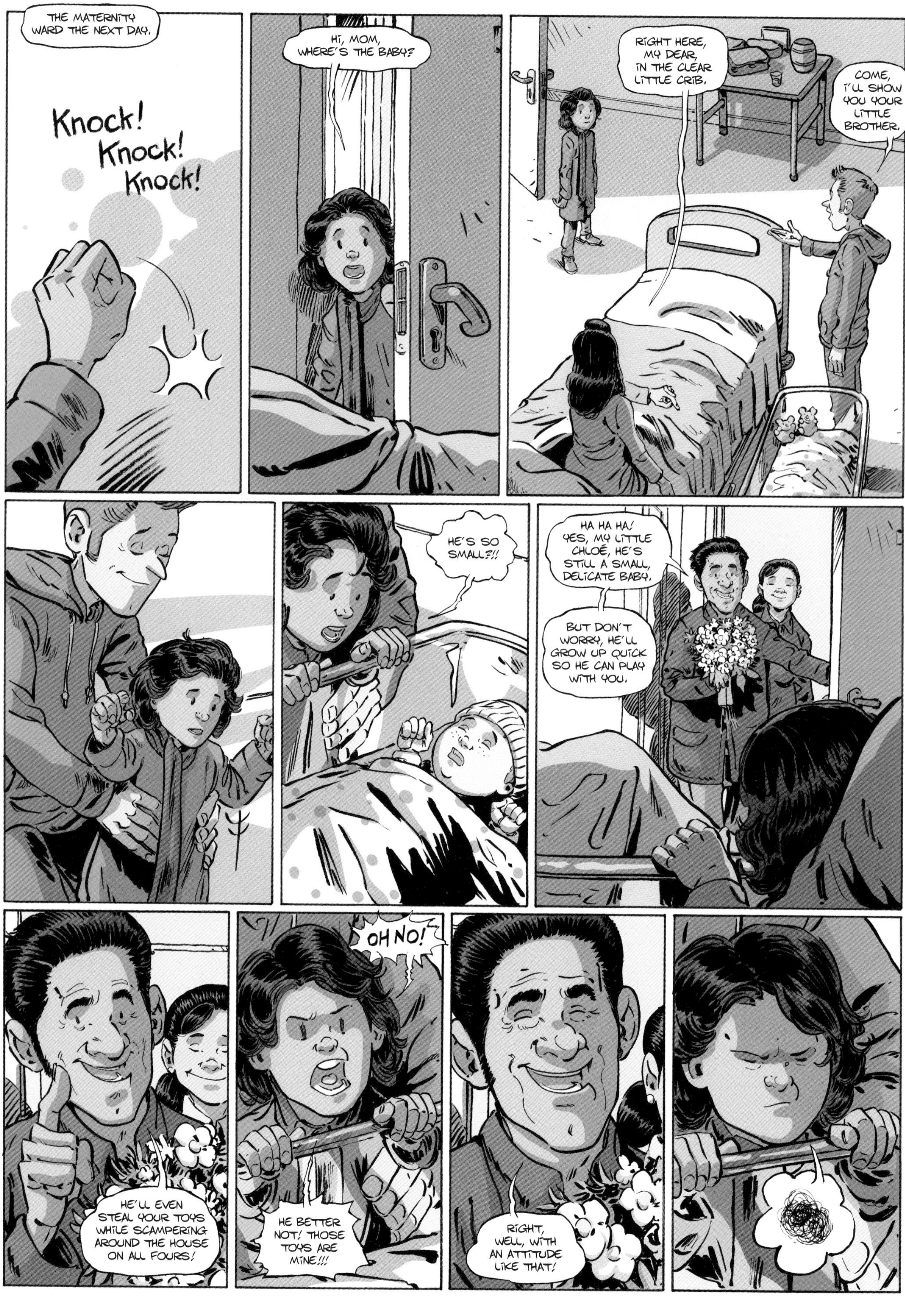
THE MATERNITY WARD THE NEXT DAY.
Knock! Knock! Knock!
HI, MOM, WHERE'S THE BABY?
RIGHT HERE, MY DEAR, IN THE CLEAR LITTLE CRIB.
COME, I'LL SHOW YOU YOUR LITTLE BROTHER.
HE'S SO SMALL?!!
HA HA HA! YES, MY LITTLE CHLOÉ, HE'S STILL A SMALL, DELICATE BABY.
BUT DON'T WORRY, HE'LL GROW UP QUICK SO HE CAN PLAY WITH YOU.
HE'LL EVEN STEAL YOUR TOYS WHILE SCAMPERING AROUND THE HOUSE ON ALL FOURS!
OH NO!
HE BETTER NOT! THOSE TOYS ARE MINE!!!
RIGHT, WELL, WITH AN ATTITUDE LIKE THAT!

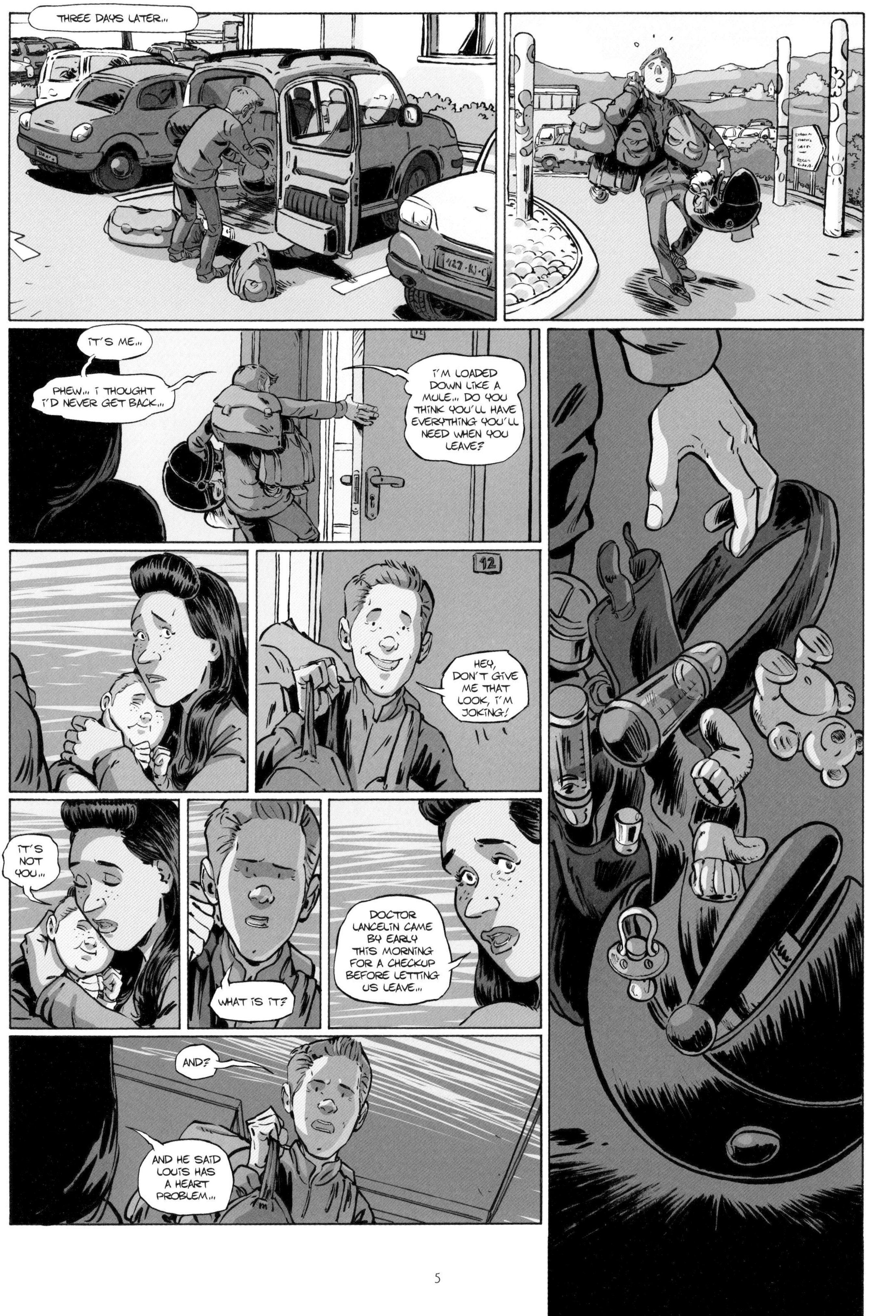
THREE DAYS LATER...
IT'S ME...
PHEW... I THOUGHT I'D NEVER GET BACK...
I'M LOADED DOWN LIKE A MULE... DO YOU THINK YOU'LL HAVE EVERYTHING YOU'LL NEED WHEN YOU LEAVE?
HEY, DON'T GIVE ME THAT LOOK, I'M JOKING!
IT'S NOT YOU...
WHAT IS IT?
DOCTOR LANCELIN CAME BY EARLY THIS MORNING FOR A CHECKUP BEFORE LETTING US LEAVE...
AND?
AND HE SAID LOUIS HAS A HEART PROBLEM...

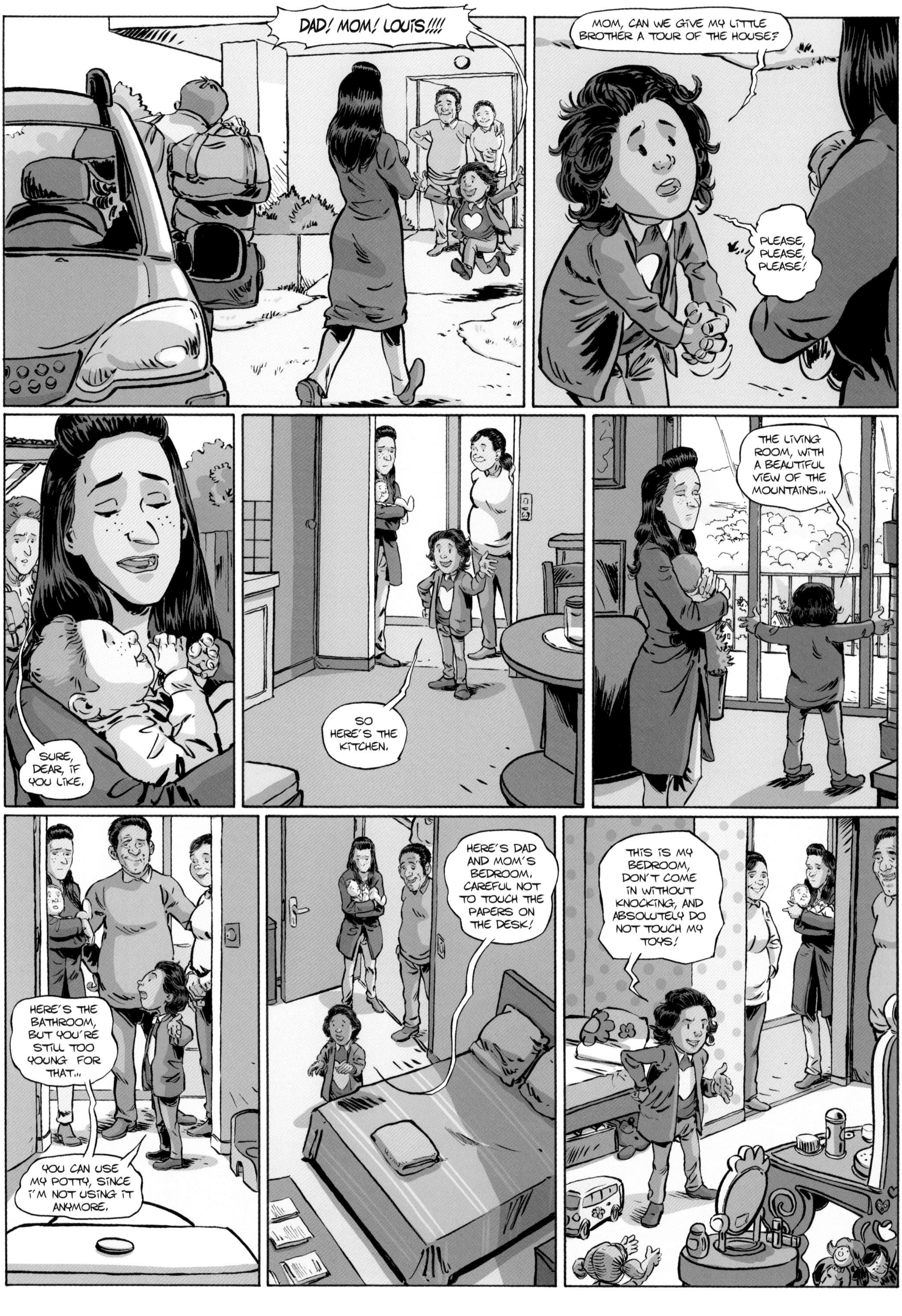
DAD! MOM! LOUIS!!!!
MOM, CAN WE GIVE MY LITTLE BROTHER A TOUR OF THE HOUSE?
PLEASE, PLEASE, PLEASE!
SURE, DEAR, IF YOU LIKE.
SO HERE'S THE KITCHEN.
THE LIVING ROOM, WITH A BEAUTIFUL VIEW OF THE MOUNTAINS...
HERE'S THE BATHROOM, BUT YOU'RE STILL TOO YOUNG FOR THAT...
YOU CAN USE MY POTTY, SINCE I'M NOT USING IT ANYMORE.
HERE'S DAD AND MOM'S BEDROOM. CAREFUL NOT TO TOUCH THE PAPERS ON THE DESK!
THIS IS MY BEDROOM, DON'T COME IN WITHOUT KNOCKING, AND ABSOLUTELY DO NOT TOUCH MY TOYS!

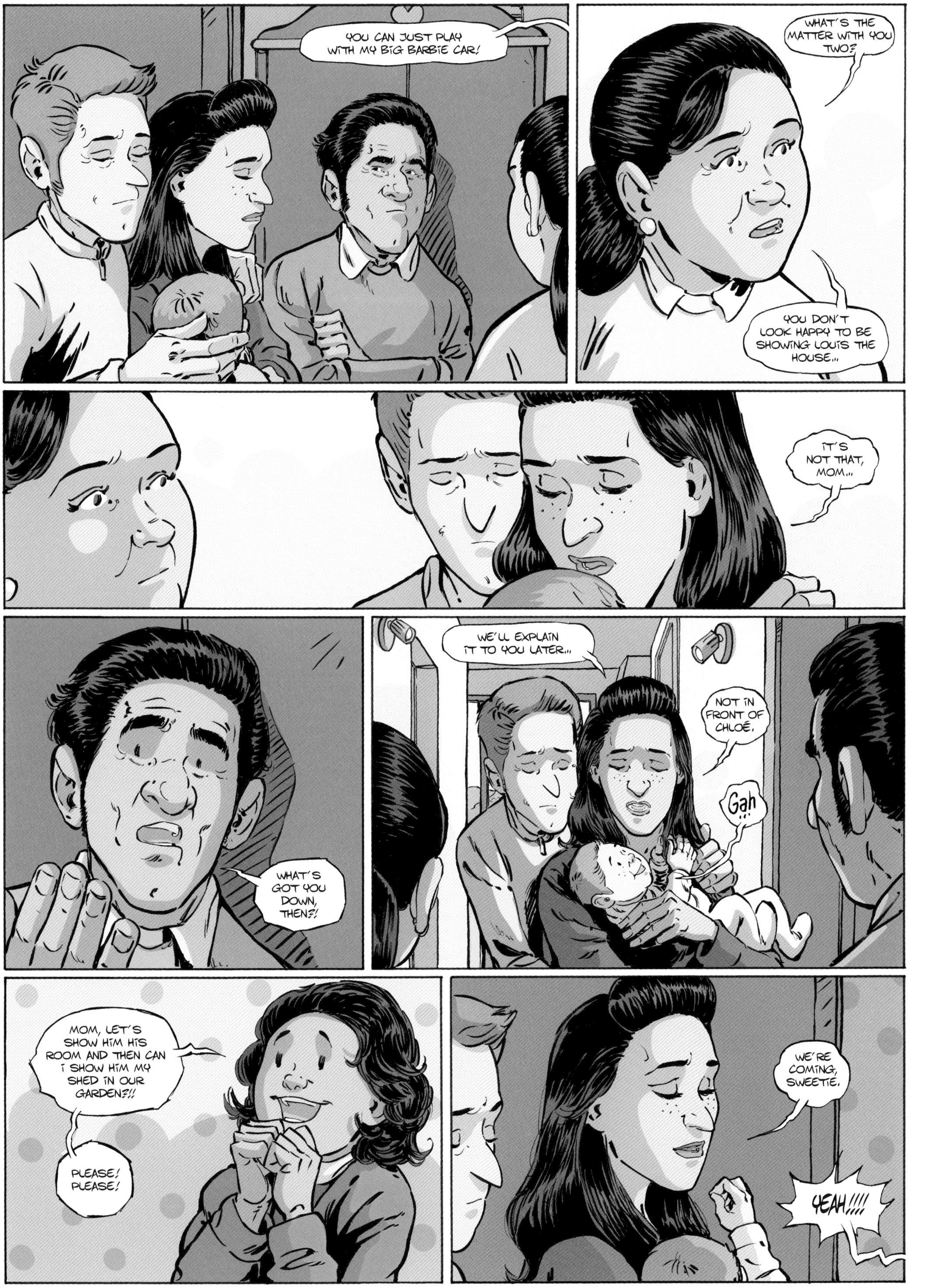
YOU CAN JUST PLAY WITH MY BIG BARBIE CAR!
WHAT'S THE MATTER WITH YOU TWO?
YOU DON'T LOOK HAPPY TO BE SHOWING LOUIS THE HOUSE...
IT'S NOT THAT, MOM...
WHAT'S GOT YOU DOWN, THEN?!
WE'LL EXPLAIN IT TO YOU LATER...
NOT IN FRONT OF CHLOÉ.
Gah
MOM, LET'S SHOW HIM HIS ROOM AND THEN CAN I SHOW HIM MY SHED IN OUR GARDEN?!!
PLEASE! PLEASE!
WE'RE COMING, SWEETIE.
YEAH!!!!

THE PEDIATRICIAN SAID IT CAN HAPPEN TO SOME BABIES AT BIRTH.

BUT HOW COULD THEY HAVE MISSED IT?

NO IDEA.

LOUIS STILL SEEMS HEALTHY, AND THE DOCTOR ALSO TOLD YOU THAT IN SOME CASES, THESE HEART PROBLEMS CAN DISAPPEAR A FEW DAYS AFTER BIRTH.

YES...

THEN I'M SURE IT'S GOING TO PASS!

THIS LITTLE GUY LOOKS SOLID AS A ROCK!

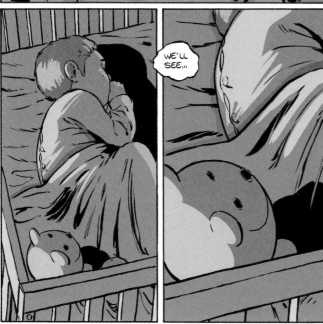

WE'LL SEE...

8

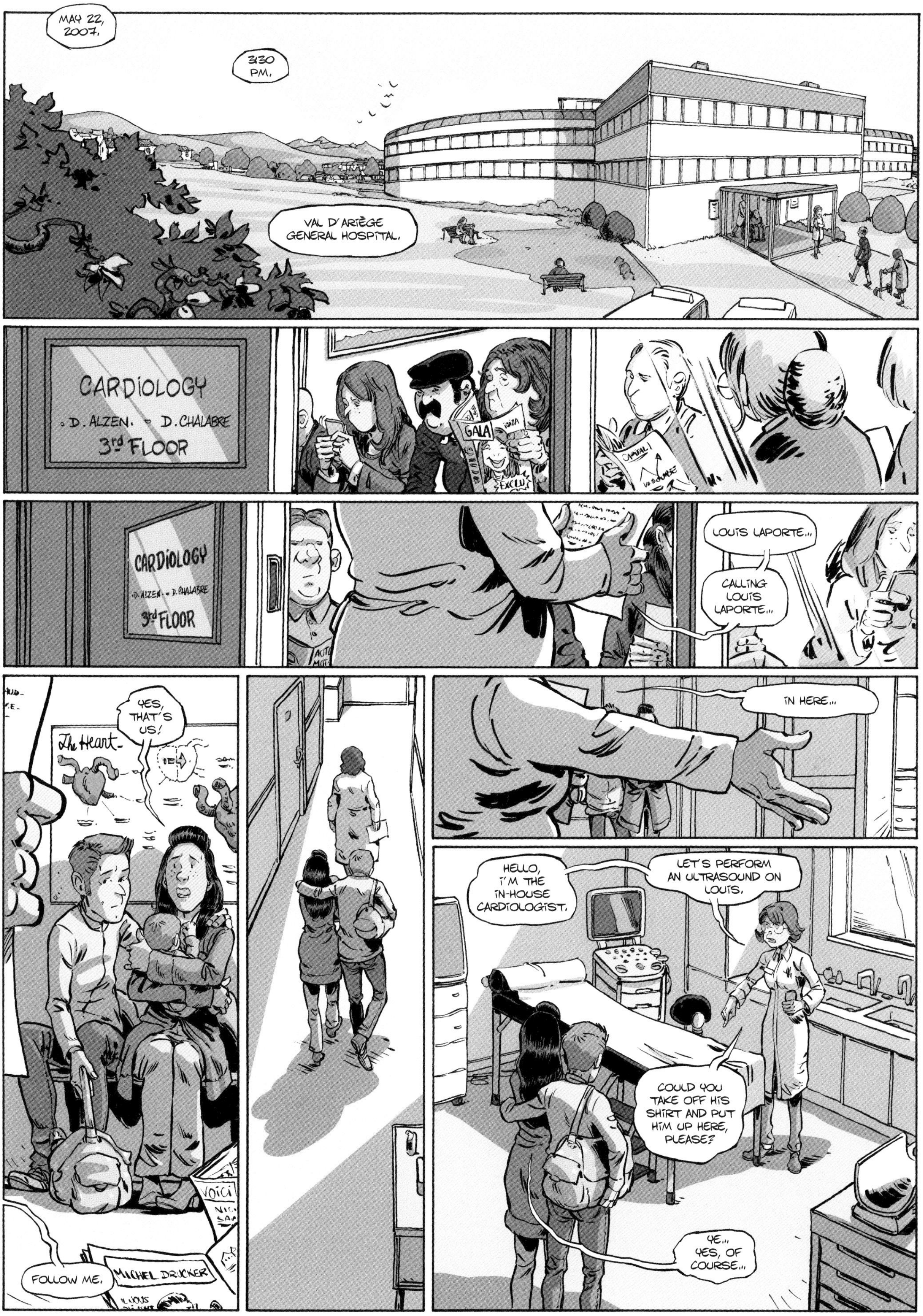
MAY 22, 2007.
3:30 PM.
VAL D'ARIÈGE GENERAL HOSPITAL.
CARDIOLOGY
D. ALZEN. D. CHALABRE
3rd FLOOR
GALA
CAPITAL
CARDIOLOGY
D. ALZEN. D. CHALABRE
3rd FLOOR
LOUIS LAPORTE...
CALLING LOUIS LAPORTE...
YES, THAT'S US!
The Heart
FOLLOW ME.
MICHEL DRUCKER
VOICI
IN HERE...
HELLO, I'M THE IN-HOUSE CARDIOLOGIST.
LET'S PERFORM AN ULTRASOUND ON LOUIS.
COULD YOU TAKE OFF HIS SHIRT AND PUT HIM UP HERE, PLEASE?
YE... YES, OF COURSE...

THUMP!

THUMP!

THUMP!

THUMP!

THUMP!

THUMP!

YES...

THERE'S DEFINITELY SOMETHING...

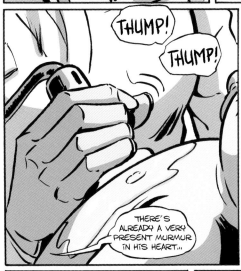

THUMP!

THUMP!

THERE'S ALREADY A VERY PRESENT MURMUR IN HIS HEART...

THUMP!

THUMP!

THAT CONFIRMS HIS CARDIAC ISSUE...

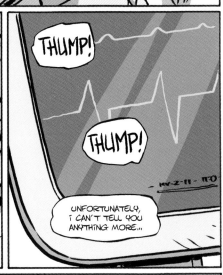

THUMP!

THUMP!

UNFORTUNATELY, I CAN'T TELL YOU ANYTHING MORE...

THE MACHINES HERE IN FOIX AREN'T POWERFUL ENOUGH...

YOU'LL HAVE TO GO TO TOULOUSE, TO THE PASTEUR CLINIC. I DID MY RESIDENCY THERE WITH PROFESSOR HALTS, ONE OF THE GREATEST SPECIALISTS IN CHILD CARDIOLOGY...

I'LL REFER YOU TO HIM ASAP, HE'LL KNOW HOW TO FIND OUT WHAT'S GOING ON. I CAN CONTACT HIM DIRECTLY, IF YOU'D LIKE, THAT'LL BUY YOU SOME TIME...

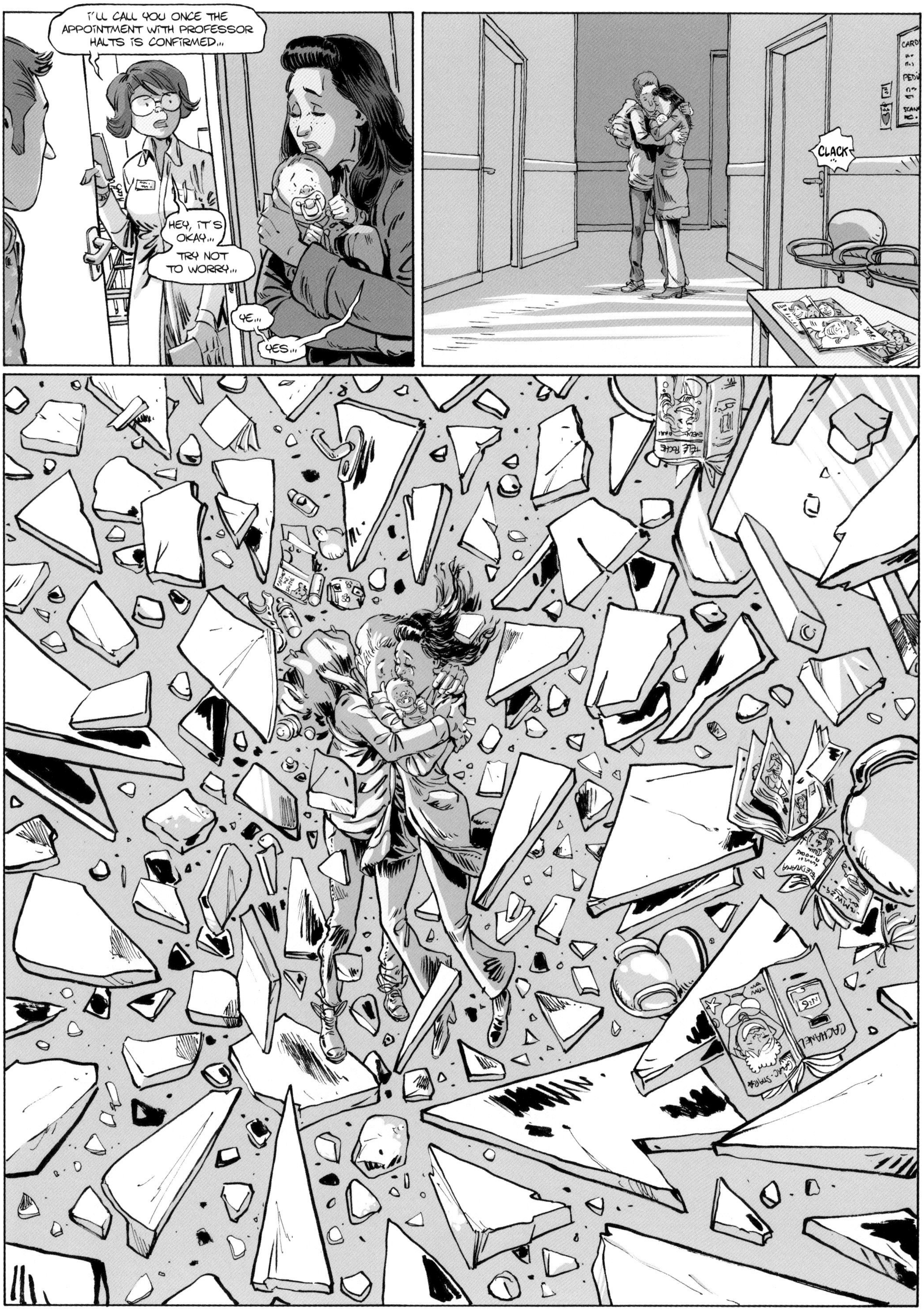
I'LL CALL YOU ONCE THE APPOINTMENT WITH PROFESSOR HALTS IS CONFIRMED...
HEY, IT'S OKAY...
TRY NOT TO WORRY...
YE...
YES...
CLACK

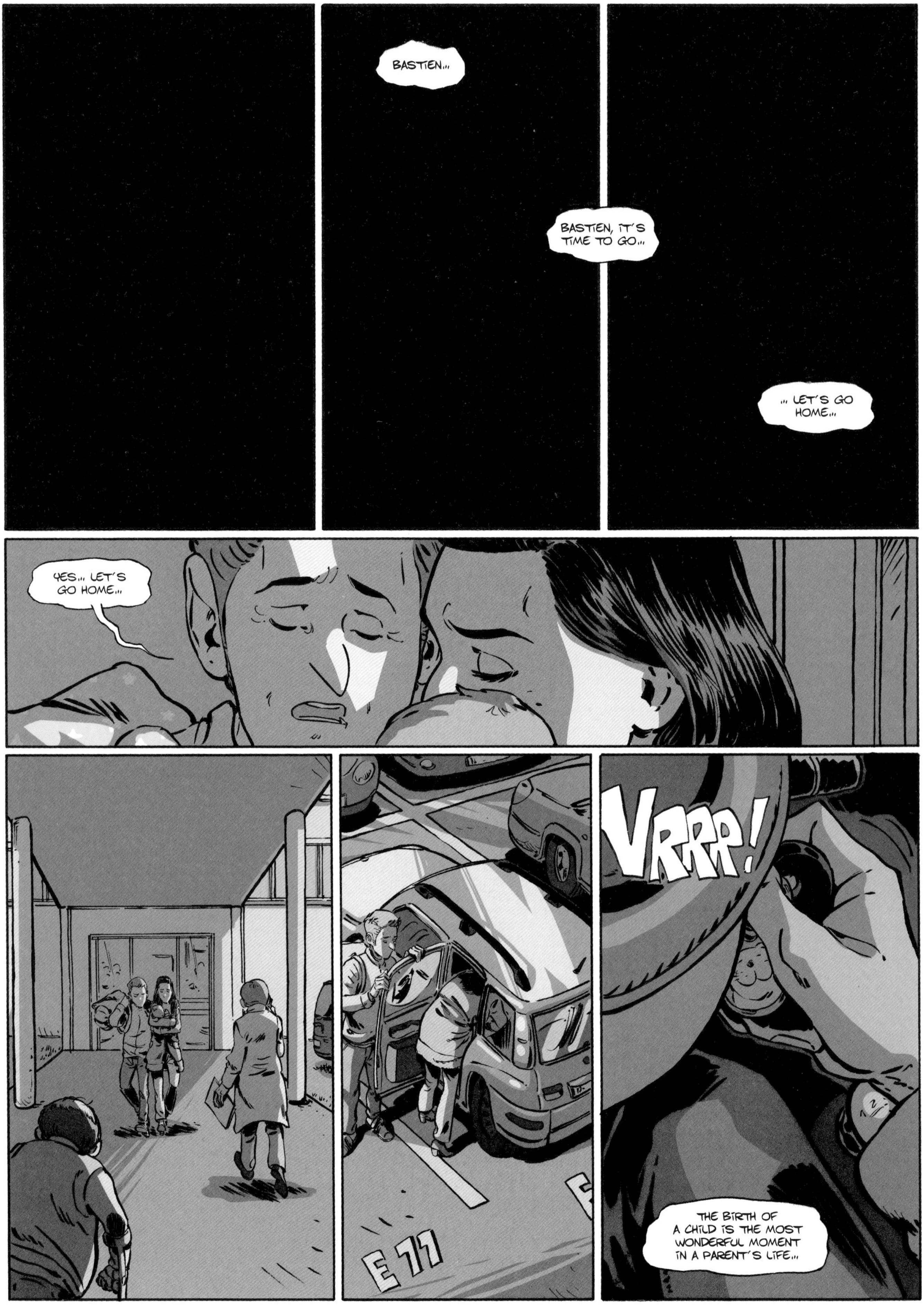
BASTIEN...
BASTIEN, IT'S TIME TO GO...
... LET'S GO HOME...
YES... LET'S GO HOME...
VRRR!
THE BIRTH OF A CHILD IS THE MOST WONDERFUL MOMENT IN A PARENT'S LIFE...

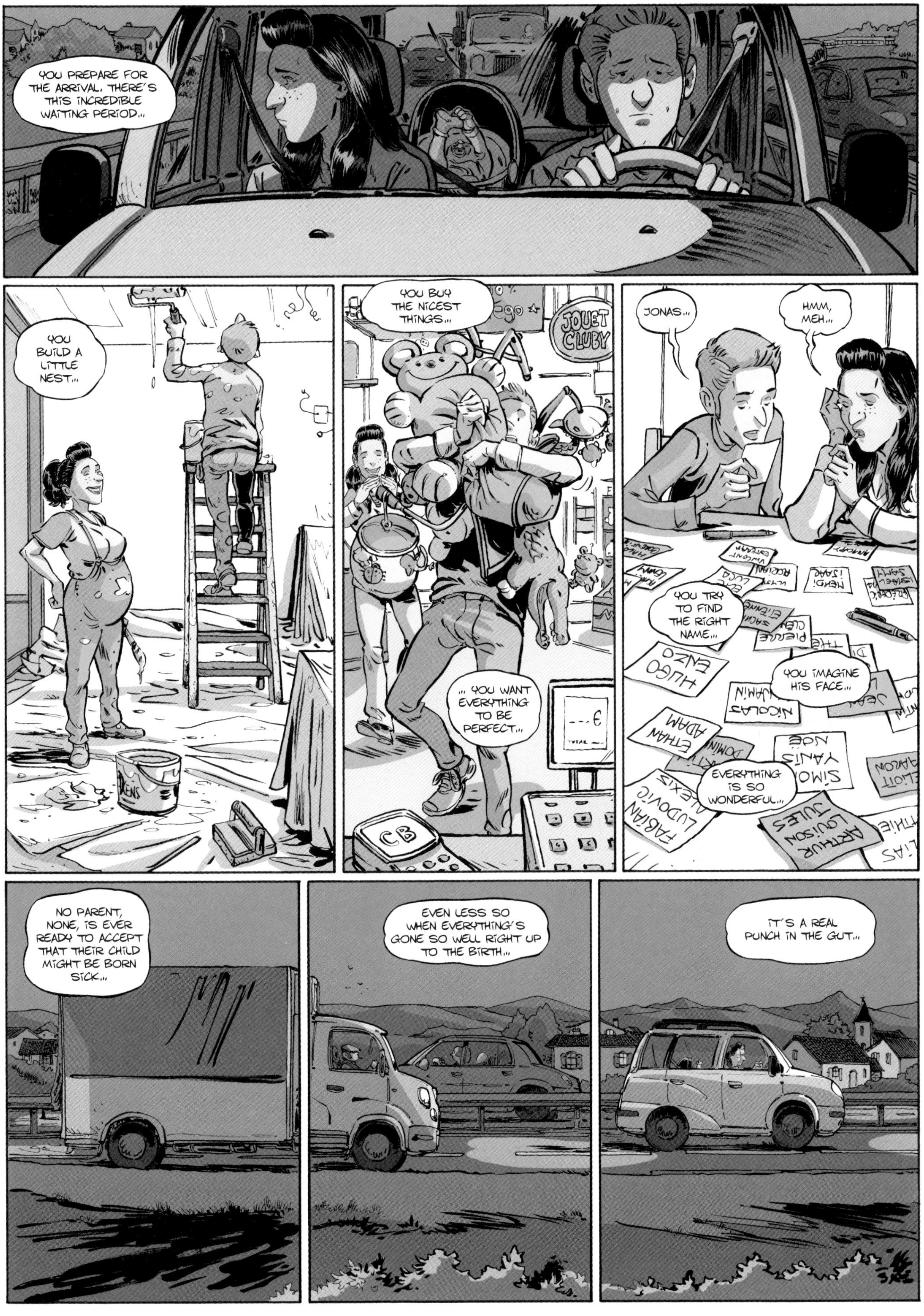
YOU PREPARE FOR THE ARRIVAL. THERE'S THIS INCREDIBLE WAITING PERIOD...
YOU BUILD A LITTLE NEST...
YOU BUY THE NICEST THINGS...
JOUET CLUBY
... YOU WANT EVERYTHING TO BE PERFECT...
CB
JONAS...
HMM, MEH...
YOU TRY TO FIND THE RIGHT NAME...
YOU IMAGINE HIS FACE...
EVERYTHING IS SO WONDERFUL...
NO PARENT, NONE, IS EVER READY TO ACCEPT THAT THEIR CHILD MIGHT BE BORN SICK...
EVEN LESS SO WHEN EVERYTHING'S GONE SO WELL RIGHT UP TO THE BIRTH...
IT'S A REAL PUNCH IN THE GUT...

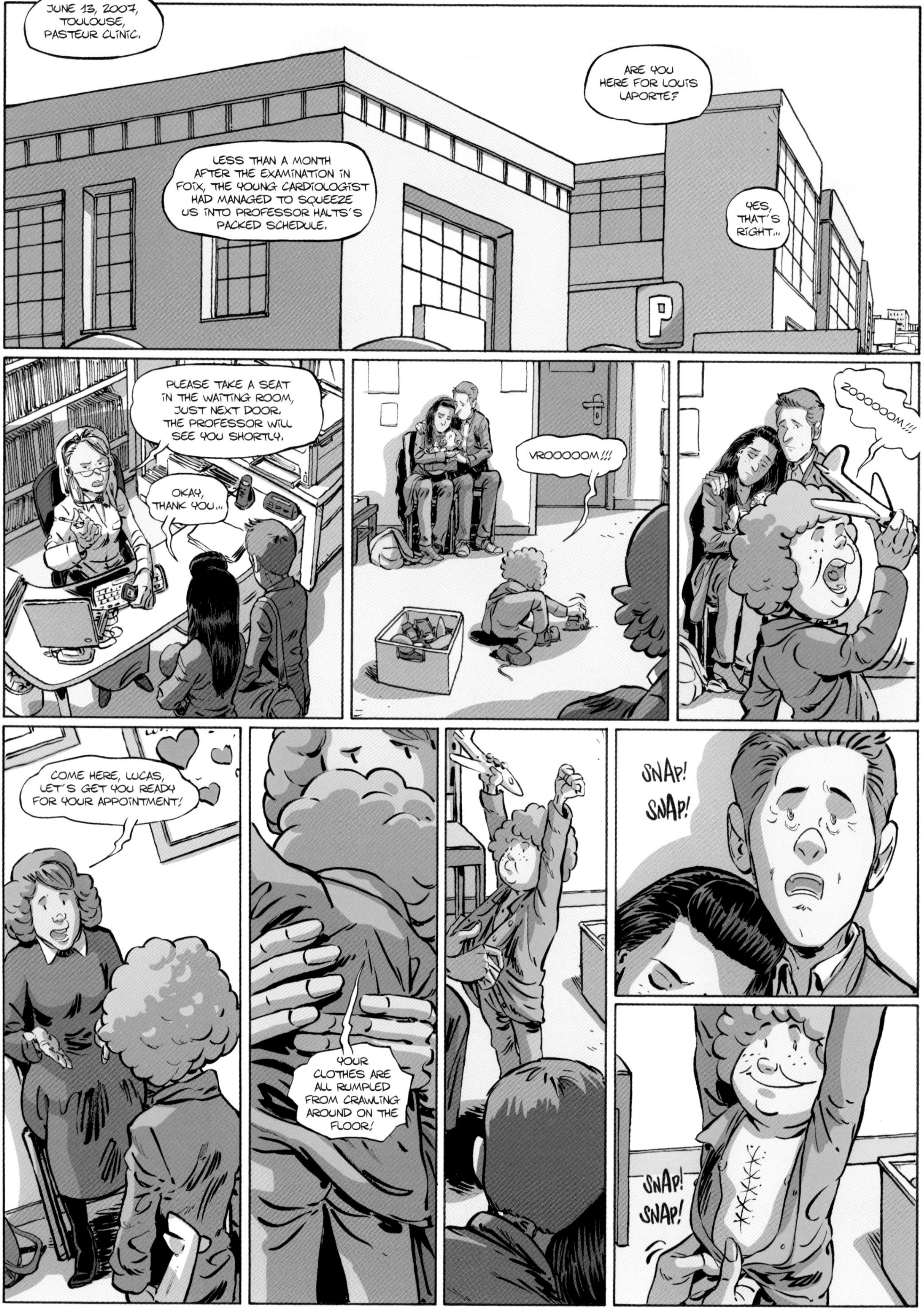
JUNE 13, 2007, TOULOUSE, PASTEUR CLINIC.
LESS THAN A MONTH AFTER THE EXAMINATION IN FOIX, THE YOUNG CARDIOLOGIST HAD MANAGED TO SQUEEZE US INTO PROFESSOR HALTS'S PACKED SCHEDULE.
ARE YOU HERE FOR LOUIS LAPORTE?
YES, THAT'S RIGHT...
PLEASE TAKE A SEAT IN THE WAITING ROOM, JUST NEXT DOOR. THE PROFESSOR WILL SEE YOU SHORTLY.
OKAY, THANK YOU...
VROOOOOM!!!
ZOOOOOOM!!!
COME HERE, LUCAS, LET'S GET YOU READY FOR YOUR APPOINTMENT!
YOUR CLOTHES ARE ALL RUMPLED FROM CRAWLING AROUND ON THE FLOOR!
SNAP!
SNAP!
SNAP!
SNAP!

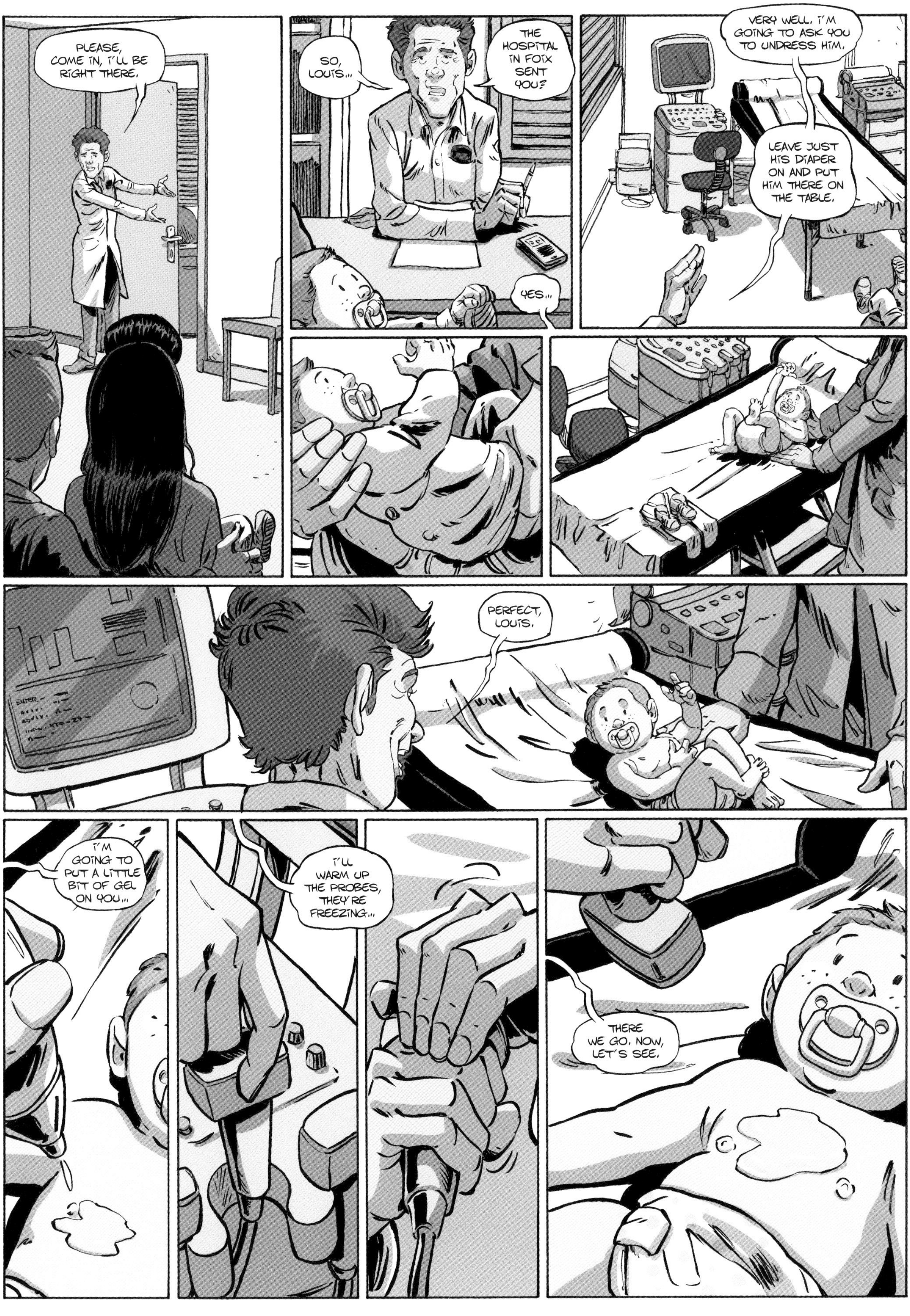
PLEASE, COME IN, I'LL BE RIGHT THERE.
SO, LOUIS...
THE HOSPITAL IN FOIX SENT YOU?
YES...
VERY WELL. I'M GOING TO ASK YOU TO UNDRESS HIM.
LEAVE JUST HIS DIAPER ON AND PUT HIM THERE ON THE TABLE.
PERFECT, LOUIS.
I'M GOING TO PUT A LITTLE BIT OF GEL ON YOU...
I'LL WARM UP THE PROBES, THEY'RE FREEZING...
THERE WE GO. NOW, LET'S SEE.

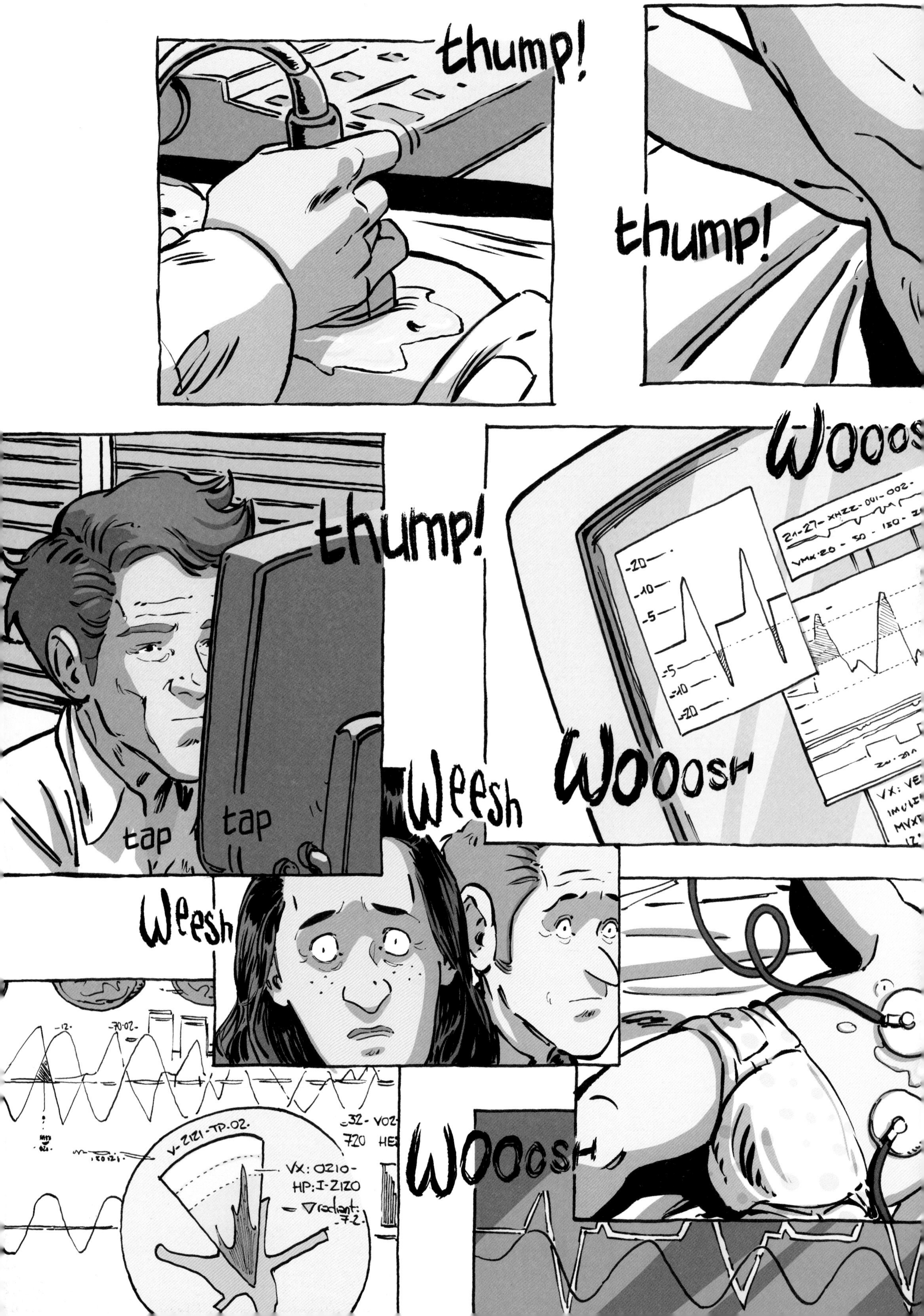
thump!
thump!
thump!
tap
tap
Wooos
WOOOSH
Weesh
Weesh
WOOOSH

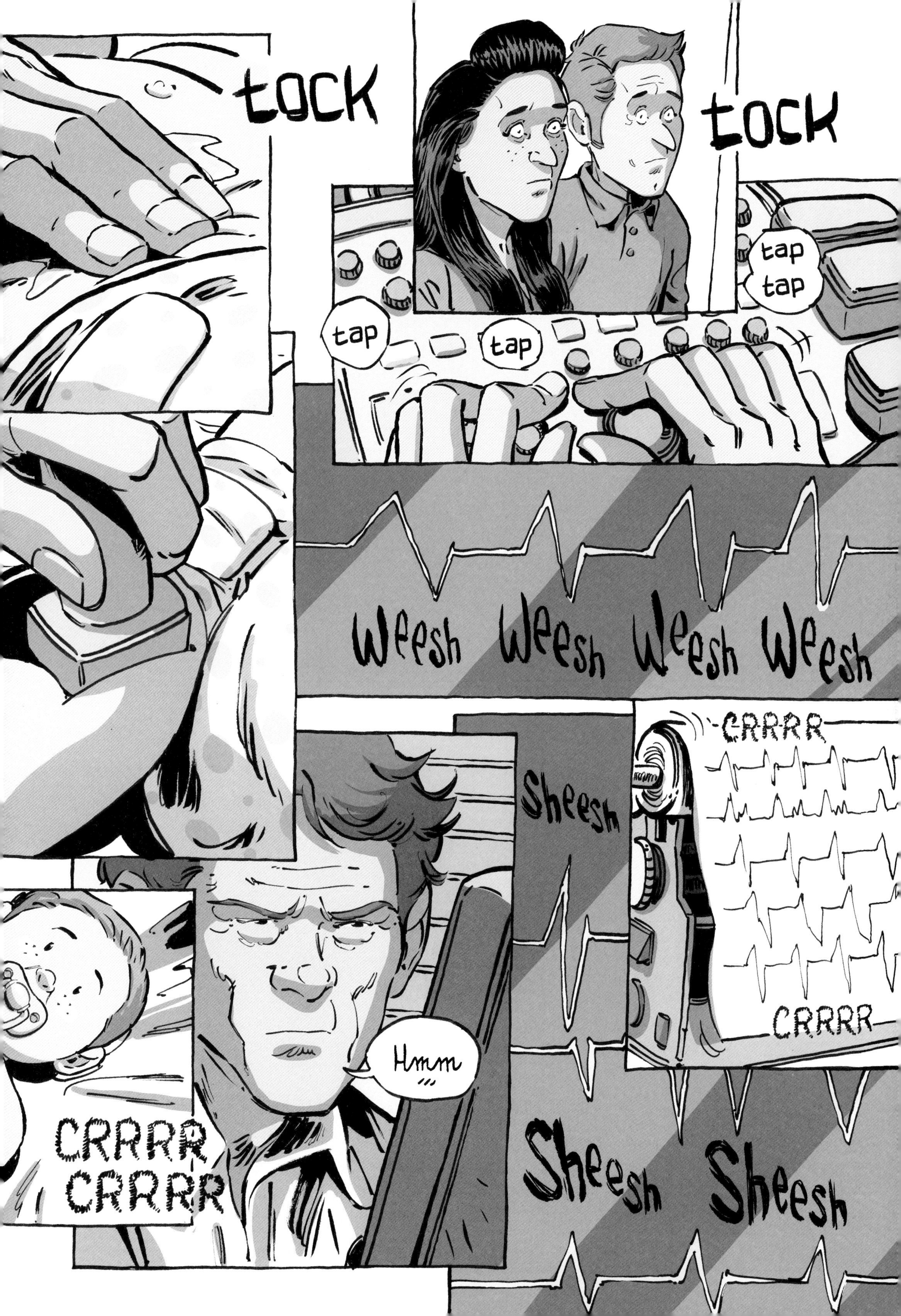
tock
tock
tap
tap
tap
tap
Weesh Weesh Weesh Weesh
CRRRR
CRRRR
Sheesh
Hmm
CRRRR
CRRRR
Sheesh Sheesh

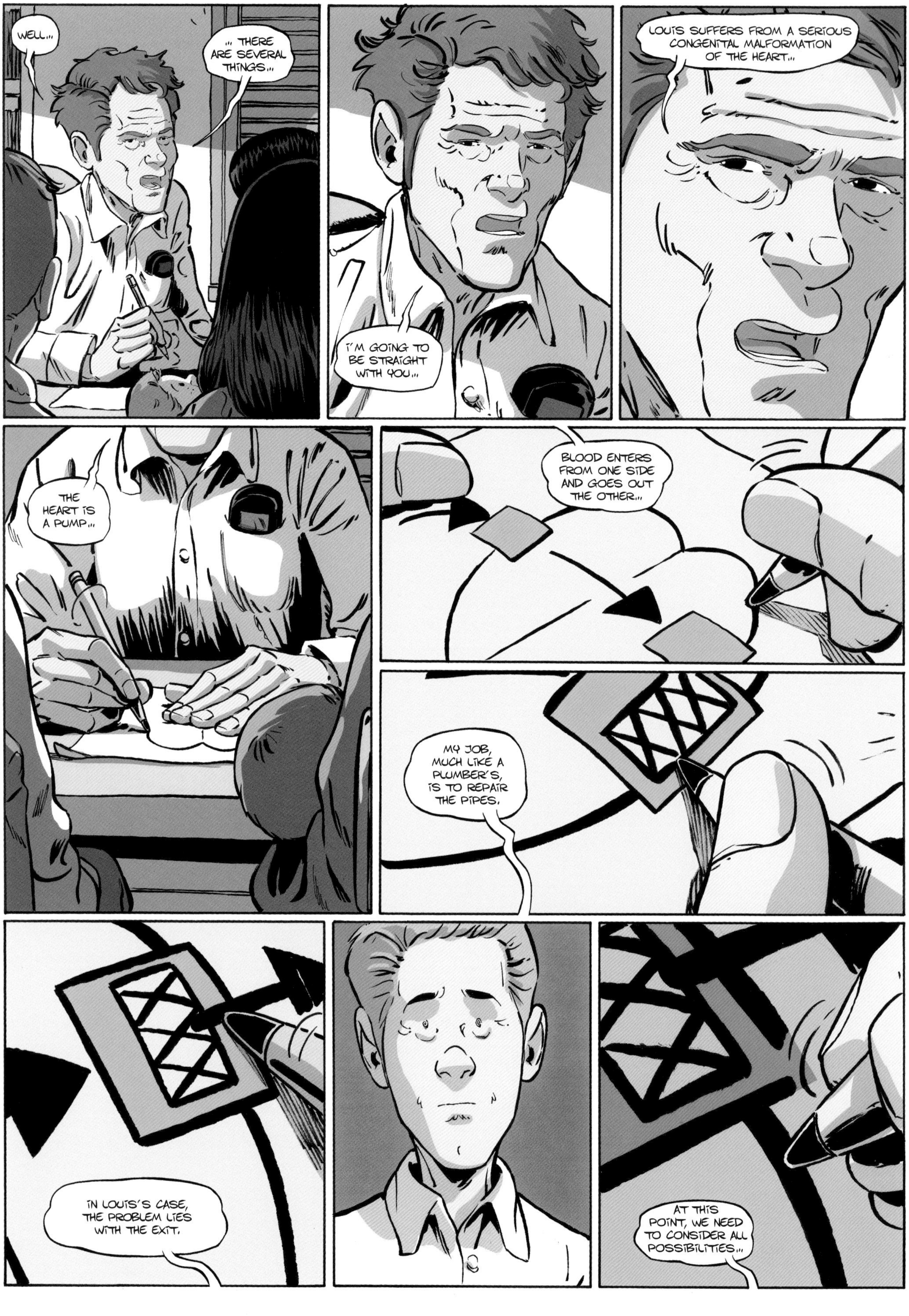
WELL...
... THERE ARE SEVERAL THINGS...
I'M GOING TO BE STRAIGHT WITH YOU...
LOUIS SUFFERS FROM A SERIOUS CONGENITAL MALFORMATION OF THE HEART...
THE HEART IS A PUMP...
BLOOD ENTERS FROM ONE SIDE AND GOES OUT THE OTHER...
MY JOB, MUCH LIKE A PLUMBER'S, IS TO REPAIR THE PIPES.
IN LOUIS'S CASE, THE PROBLEM LIES WITH THE EXIT.
AT THIS POINT, WE NEED TO CONSIDER ALL POSSIBILITIES...

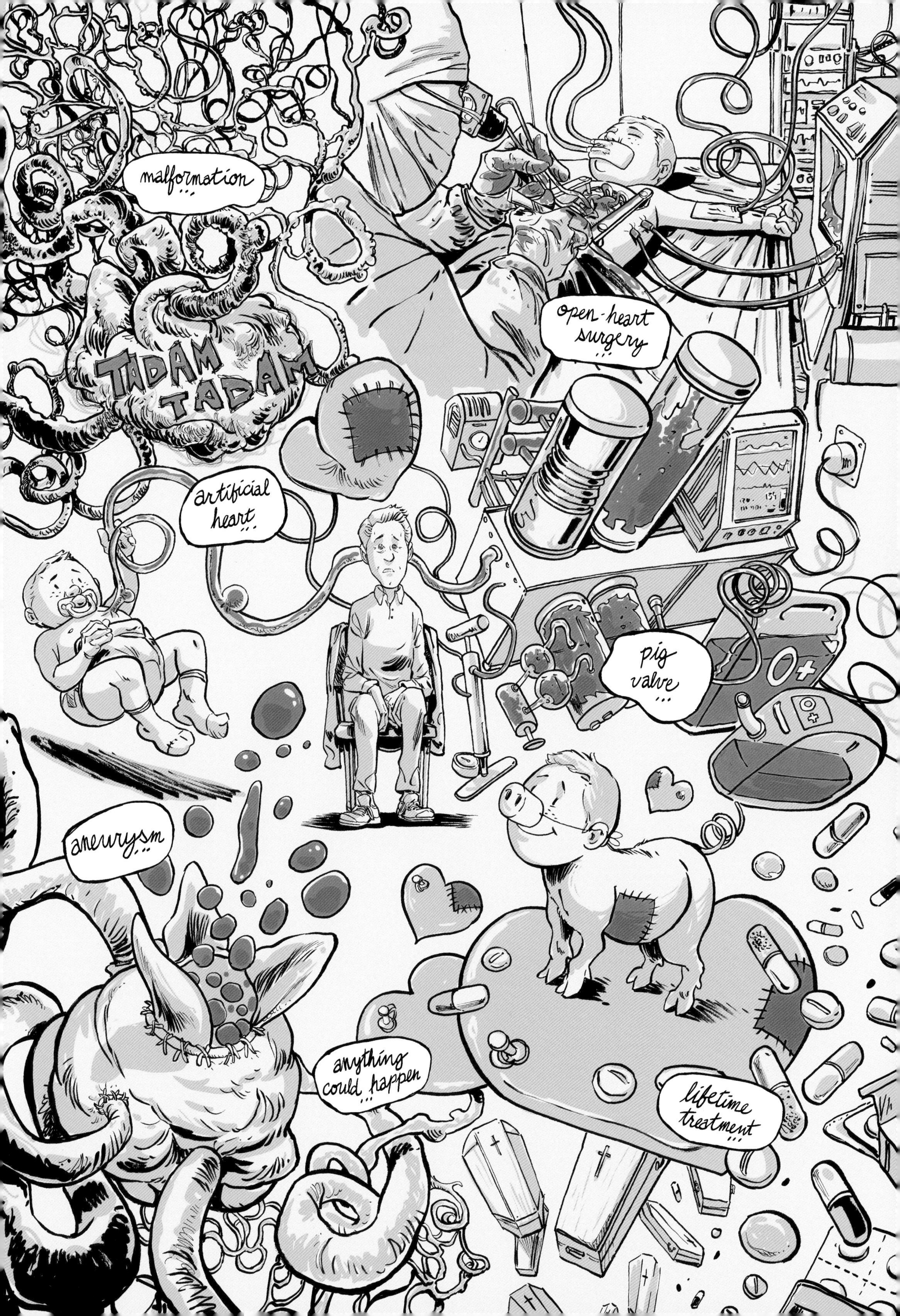
malformation...
TADAM TADAM
open-heart surgery...
artificial heart...
pig valve...
0+
aneurysm...
anything could happen...
lifetime treatment...

20

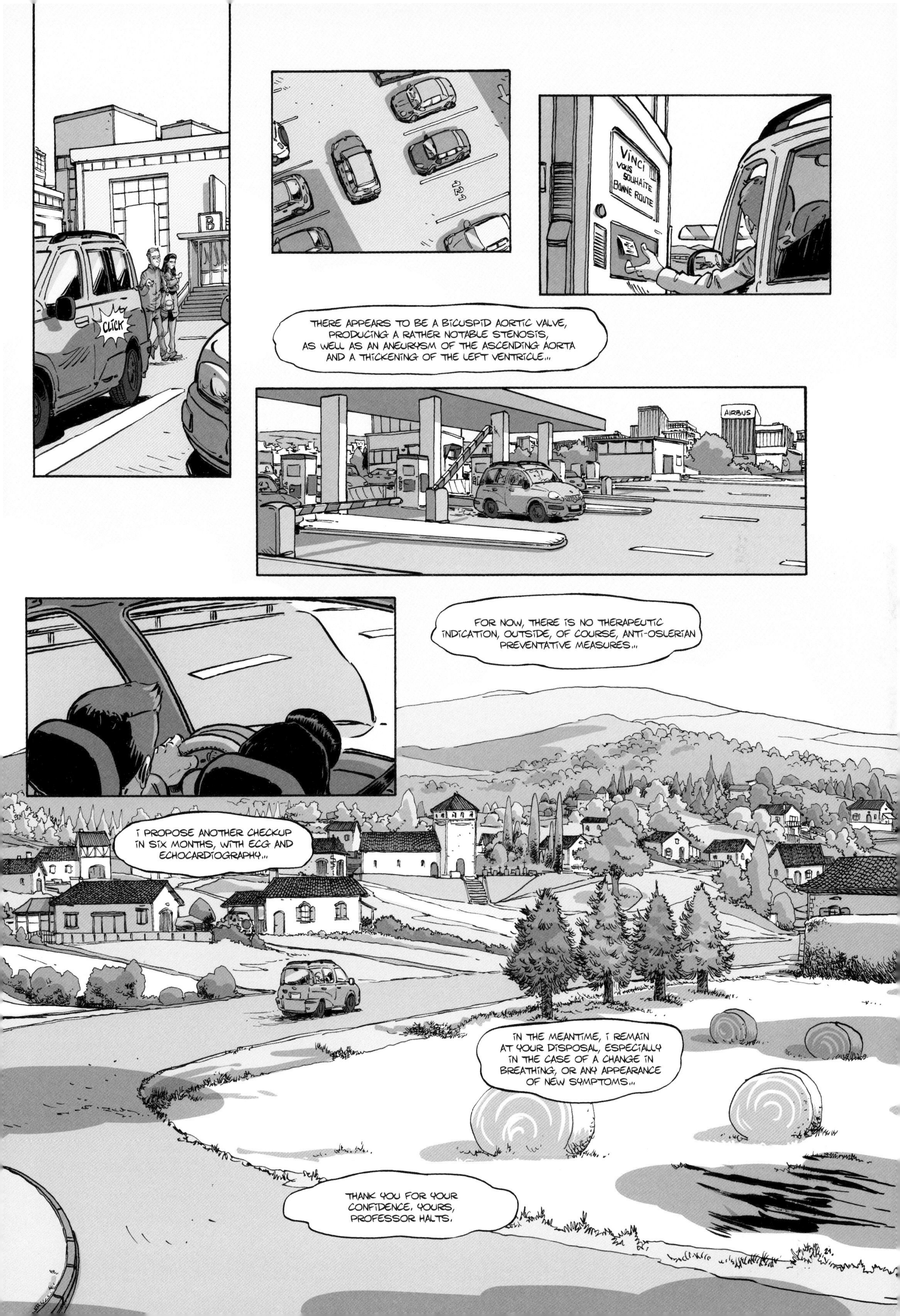
CLICK
VINCI VOUS SOUHAITE BONNE ROUTE
THERE APPEARS TO BE A BICUSPID AORTIC VALVE, PRODUCING A RATHER NOTABLE STENOSIS, AS WELL AS AN ANEURYSM OF THE ASCENDING AORTA AND A THICKENING OF THE LEFT VENTRICLE...
AIRBUS
FOR NOW, THERE IS NO THERAPEUTIC INDICATION, OUTSIDE, OF COURSE, ANTI-OSLERIAN PREVENTATIVE MEASURES...
I PROPOSE ANOTHER CHECKUP IN SIX MONTHS, WITH ECG AND ECHOCARDIOGRAPHY...
IN THE MEANTIME, I REMAIN AT YOUR DISPOSAL, ESPECIALLY IN THE CASE OF A CHANGE IN BREATHING, OR ANY APPEARANCE OF NEW SYMPTOMS...
THANK YOU FOR YOUR CONFIDENCE. YOURS, PROFESSOR HALTS.

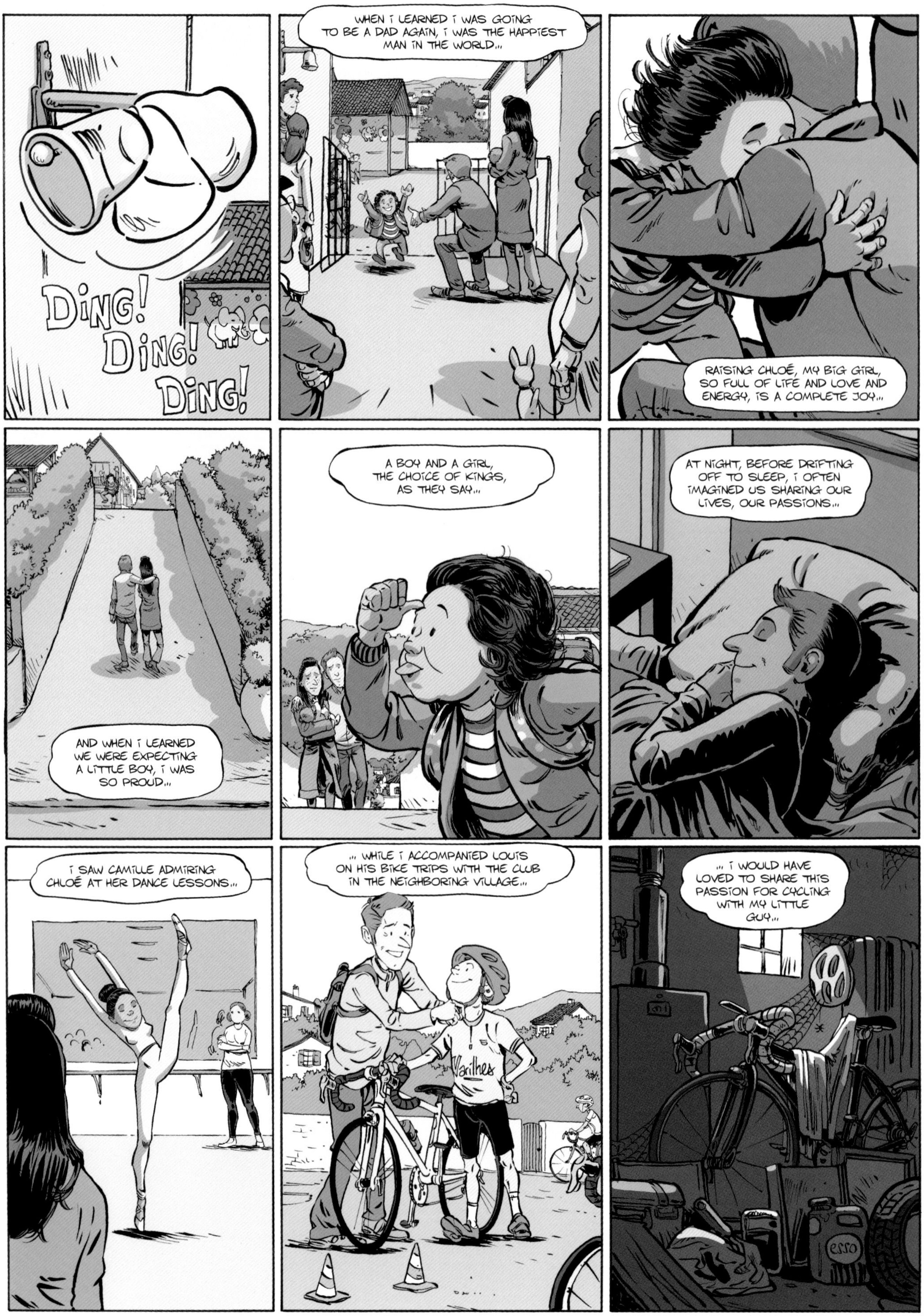
DING! DING! DING!
WHEN I LEARNED I WAS GOING TO BE A DAD AGAIN, I WAS THE HAPPIEST MAN IN THE WORLD...
RAISING CHLOÉ, MY BIG GIRL, SO FULL OF LIFE AND LOVE AND ENERGY, IS A COMPLETE JOY...
AND WHEN I LEARNED WE WERE EXPECTING A LITTLE BOY, I WAS SO PROUD...
A BOY AND A GIRL, THE CHOICE OF KINGS, AS THEY SAY...
AT NIGHT, BEFORE DRIFTING OFF TO SLEEP, I OFTEN IMAGINED US SHARING OUR LIVES, OUR PASSIONS...
I SAW CAMILLE ADMIRING CHLOÉ AT HER DANCE LESSONS...
... WHILE I ACCOMPANIED LOUIS ON HIS BIKE TRIPS WITH THE CLUB IN THE NEIGHBORING VILLAGE...
... I WOULD HAVE LOVED TO SHARE THIS PASSION FOR CYCLING WITH MY LITTLE GUY...

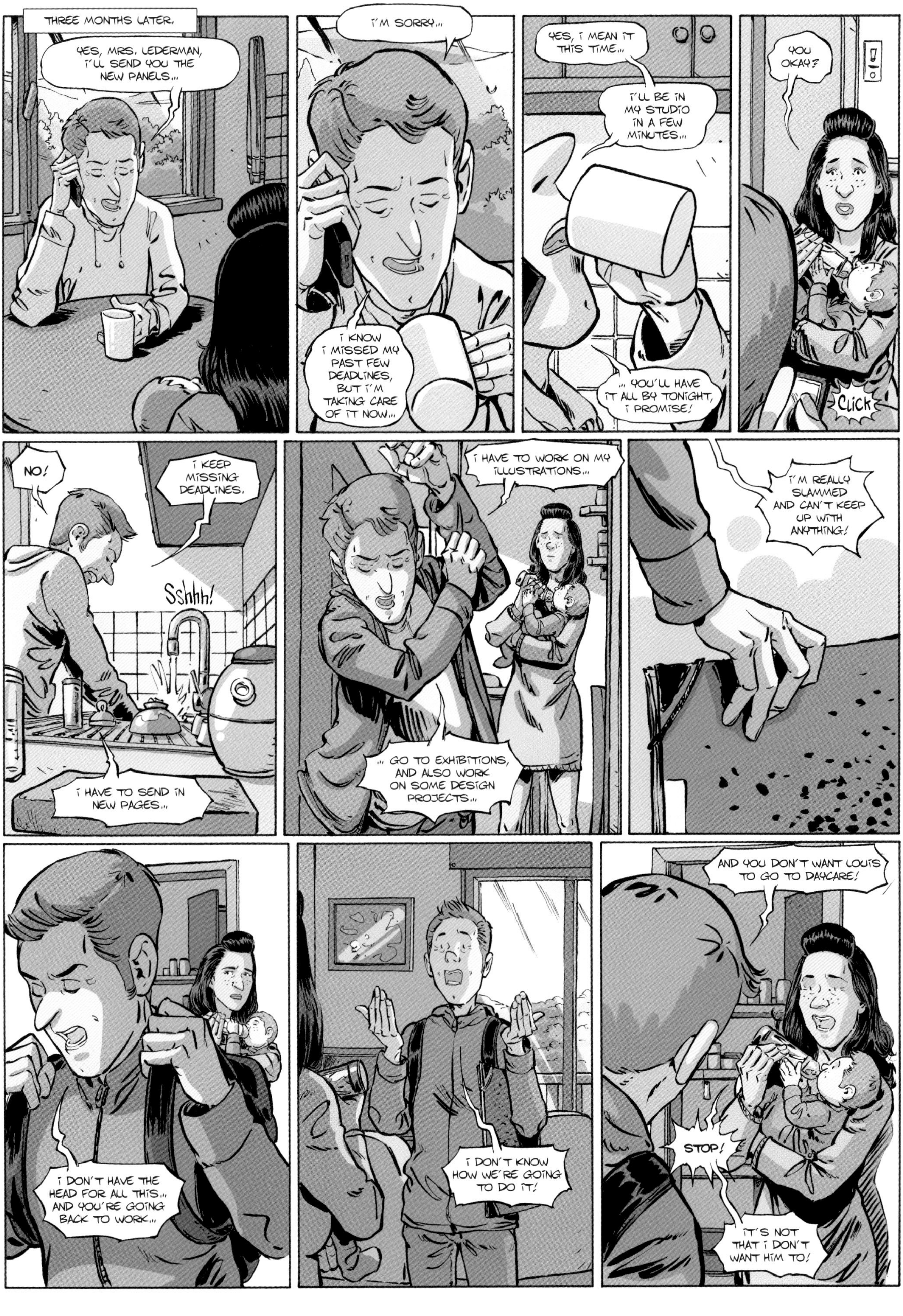
THREE MONTHS LATER.
YES, MRS. LEDERMAN, I'LL SEND YOU THE NEW PANELS...
I'M SORRY...
I KNOW I MISSED MY PAST FEW DEADLINES, BUT I'M TAKING CARE OF IT NOW...
YES, I MEAN IT THIS TIME...
I'LL BE IN MY STUDIO IN A FEW MINUTES...
... YOU'LL HAVE IT ALL BY TONIGHT, I PROMISE!
YOU OKAY?
CLICK
NO!
I KEEP MISSING DEADLINES.
Sshhh!
I HAVE TO SEND IN NEW PAGES...
I HAVE TO WORK ON MY ILLUSTRATIONS...
... GO TO EXHIBITIONS, AND ALSO WORK ON SOME DESIGN PROJECTS...
I'M REALLY SLAMMED AND CAN'T KEEP UP WITH ANYTHING!
I DON'T HAVE THE HEAD FOR ALL THIS... AND YOU'RE GOING BACK TO WORK...
I DON'T KNOW HOW WE'RE GOING TO DO IT!
AND YOU DON'T WANT LOUIS TO GO TO DAYCARE!
STOP!
IT'S NOT THAT I DON'T WANT HIM TO!

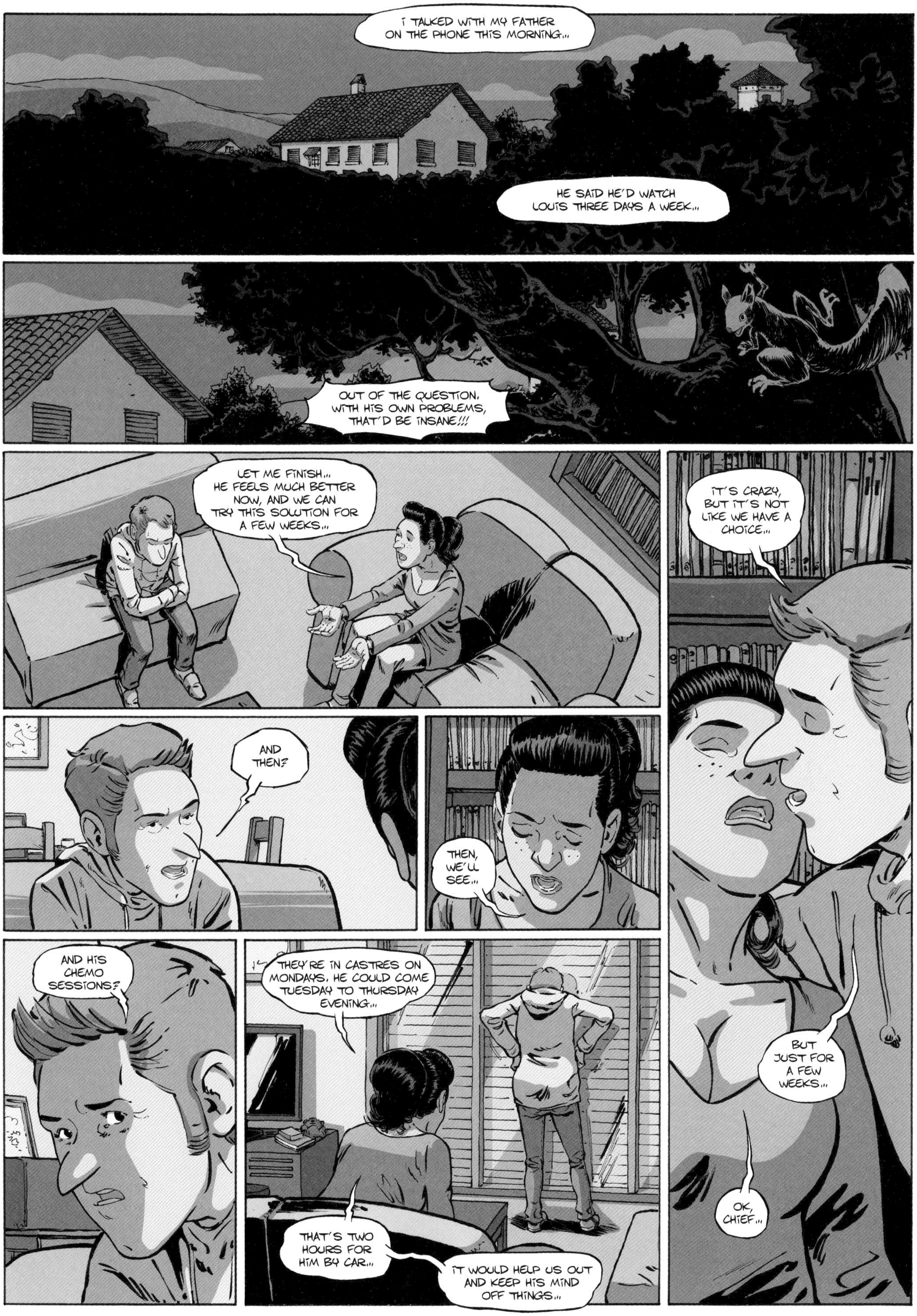
I TALKED WITH MY FATHER ON THE PHONE THIS MORNING...
HE SAID HE'D WATCH LOUIS THREE DAYS A WEEK...
OUT OF THE QUESTION. WITH HIS OWN PROBLEMS, THAT'D BE INSANE!!!
LET ME FINISH... HE FEELS MUCH BETTER NOW, AND WE CAN TRY THIS SOLUTION FOR A FEW WEEKS...
AND THEN?
THEN, WE'LL SEE...
IT'S CRAZY, BUT IT'S NOT LIKE WE HAVE A CHOICE...
BUT JUST FOR A FEW WEEKS...
OK, CHIEF...
AND HIS CHEMO SESSIONS?
THEY'RE IN CASTRES ON MONDAYS. HE COULD COME TUESDAY TO THURSDAY EVENING...
THAT'S TWO HOURS FOR HIM BY CAR...
IT WOULD HELP US OUT AND KEEP HIS MIND OFF THINGS...

SEE THAT, BIG GUY? THAT'S A COW.
MOOOO!!
OOOO!!
WHAT'S FOR LUNCH?
GREEN PEAS...
I KNOW HOW MUCH YOU LOVE THEM!
SSHHH...
UGH!!! NO!!!
I HATE THEM!!!
JUUUUUUST KIDDING!!! I'M MAKING YOU NOODLES WITH SAUSAGE!
YEAH!!! I LOVE THAT!!!
AND IT MAKES YOU STRONG!!!

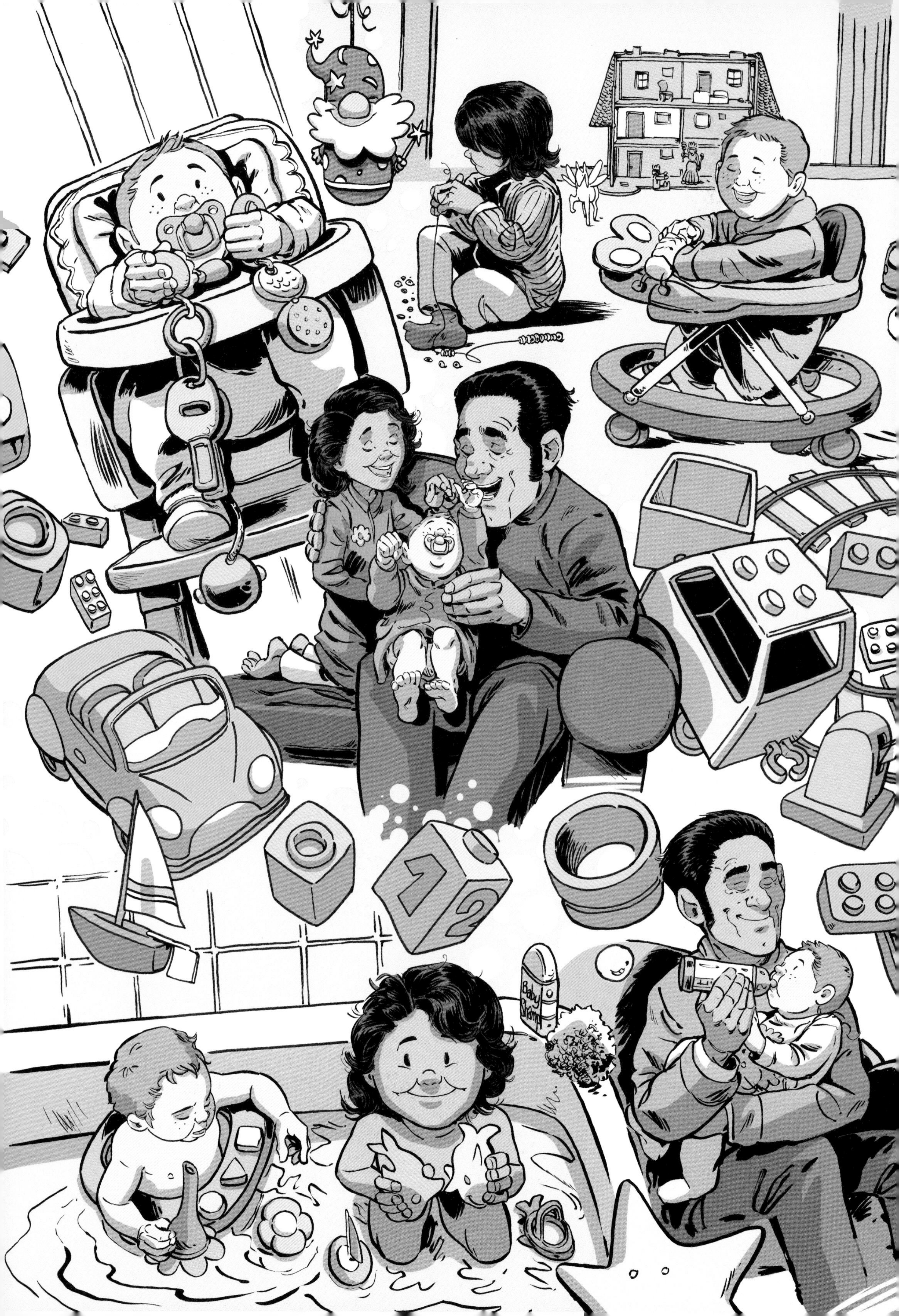
Baby
Shamp

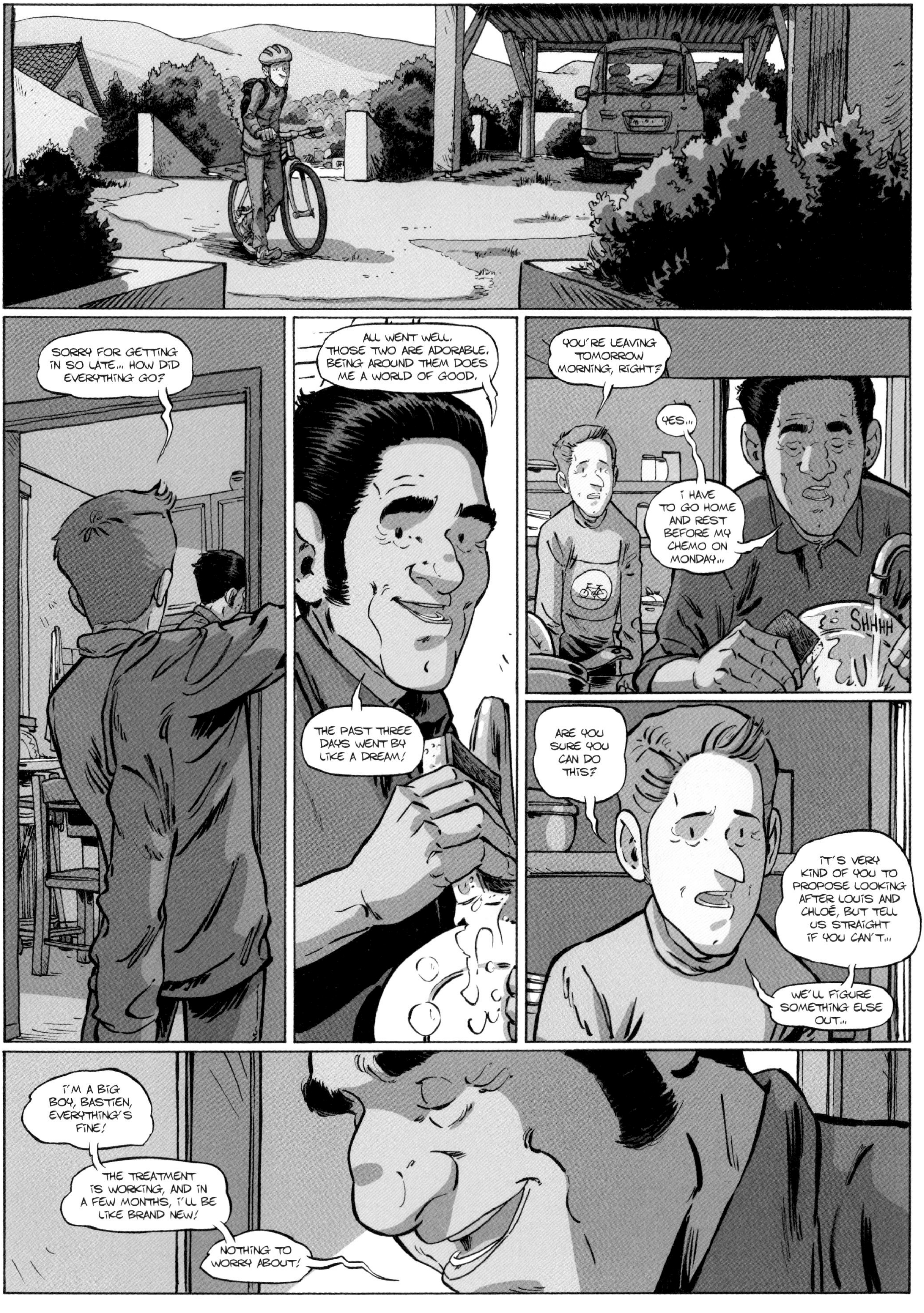
SORRY FOR GETTING IN SO LATE... HOW DID EVERYTHING GO?
ALL WENT WELL. THOSE TWO ARE ADORABLE. BEING AROUND THEM DOES ME A WORLD OF GOOD.
THE PAST THREE DAYS WENT BY LIKE A DREAM!
YOU'RE LEAVING TOMORROW MORNING, RIGHT?
YES...
I HAVE TO GO HOME AND REST BEFORE MY CHEMO ON MONDAY...
SHHHH
ARE YOU SURE YOU CAN DO THIS?
IT'S VERY KIND OF YOU TO PROPOSE LOOKING AFTER LOUIS AND CHLOÉ, BUT TELL US STRAIGHT IF YOU CAN'T...
WE'LL FIGURE SOMETHING ELSE OUT...
I'M A BIG BOY, BASTIEN, EVERYTHING'S FINE!
THE TREATMENT IS WORKING, AND IN A FEW MONTHS, I'LL BE LIKE BRAND NEW!
NOTHING TO WORRY ABOUT!

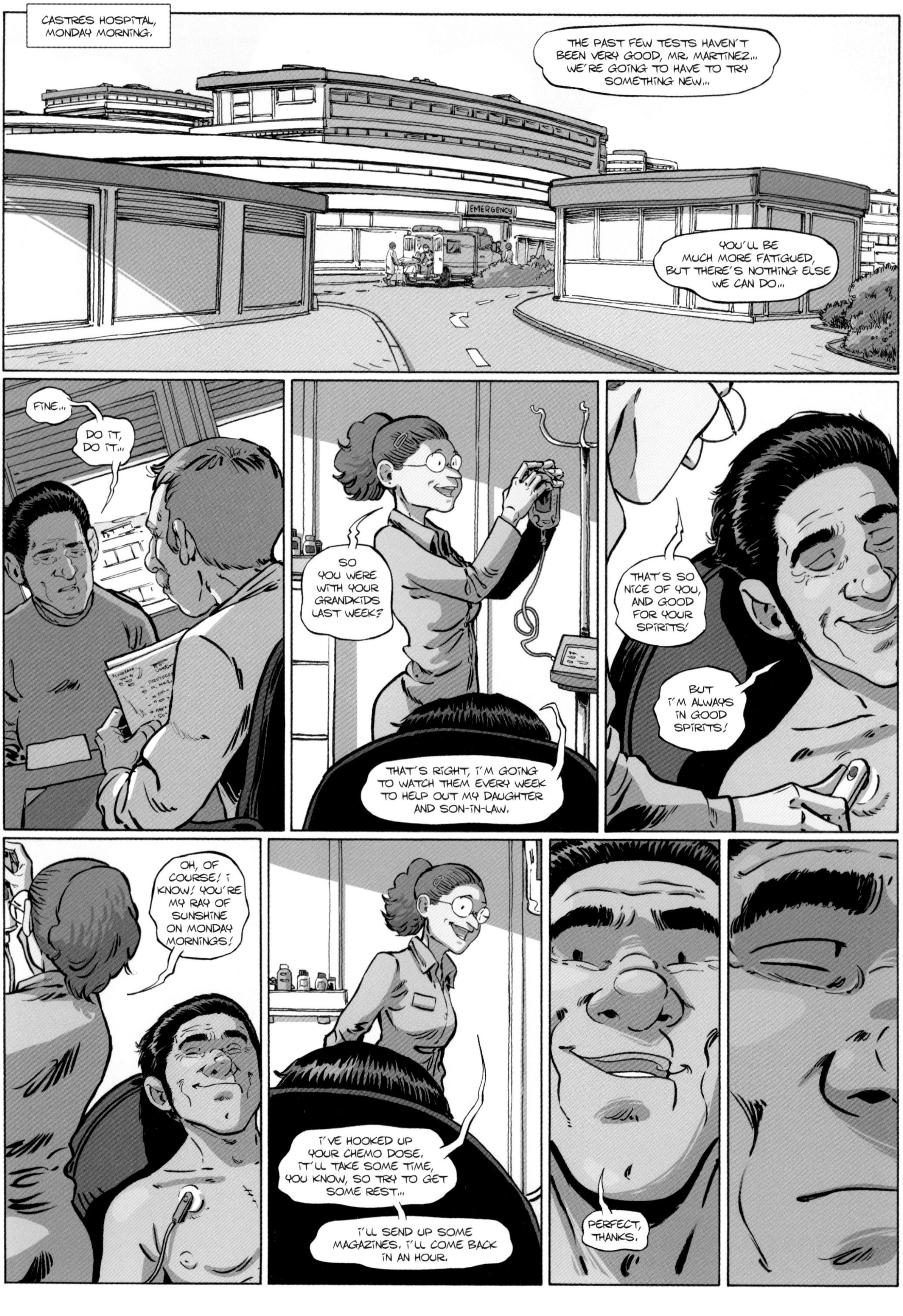
CASTRES HOSPITAL, MONDAY MORNING.
EMERGENCY
THE PAST FEW TESTS HAVEN'T BEEN VERY GOOD, MR. MARTINEZ... WE'RE GOING TO HAVE TO TRY SOMETHING NEW...
YOU'LL BE MUCH MORE FATIGUED, BUT THERE'S NOTHING ELSE WE CAN DO...
FINE...
DO IT, DO IT...
SO YOU WERE WITH YOUR GRANDKIDS LAST WEEK?
THAT'S RIGHT, I'M GOING TO WATCH THEM EVERY WEEK TO HELP OUT MY DAUGHTER AND SON-IN-LAW.
THAT'S SO NICE OF YOU, AND GOOD FOR YOUR SPIRITS!
BUT I'M ALWAYS IN GOOD SPIRITS!
OH, OF COURSE! I KNOW! YOU'RE MY RAY OF SUNSHINE ON MONDAY MORNINGS!
I'VE HOOKED UP YOUR CHEMO DOSE. IT'LL TAKE SOME TIME, YOU KNOW, SO TRY TO GET SOME REST...
I'LL SEND UP SOME MAGAZINES. I'LL COME BACK IN AN HOUR.
PERFECT, THANKS.

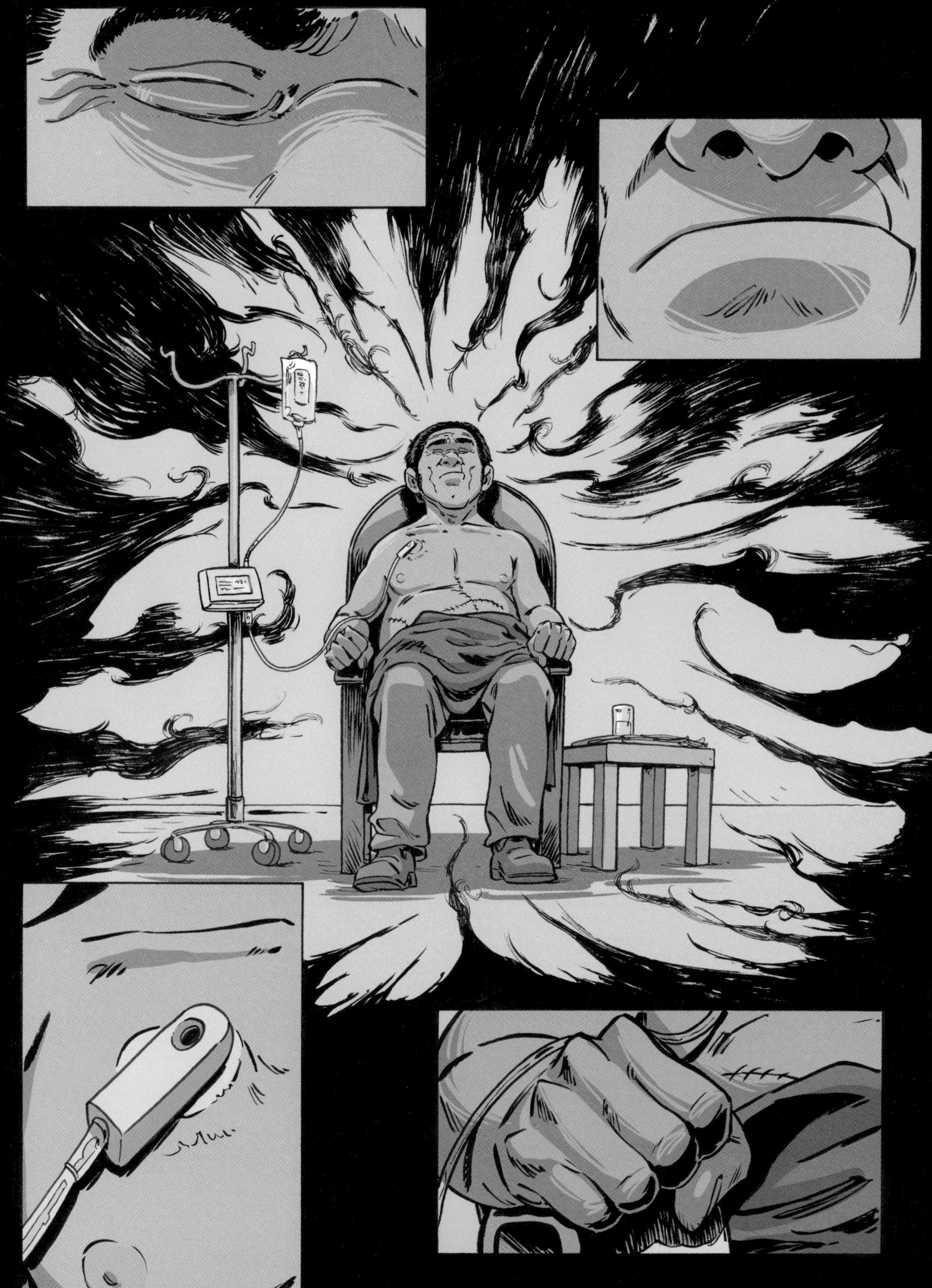

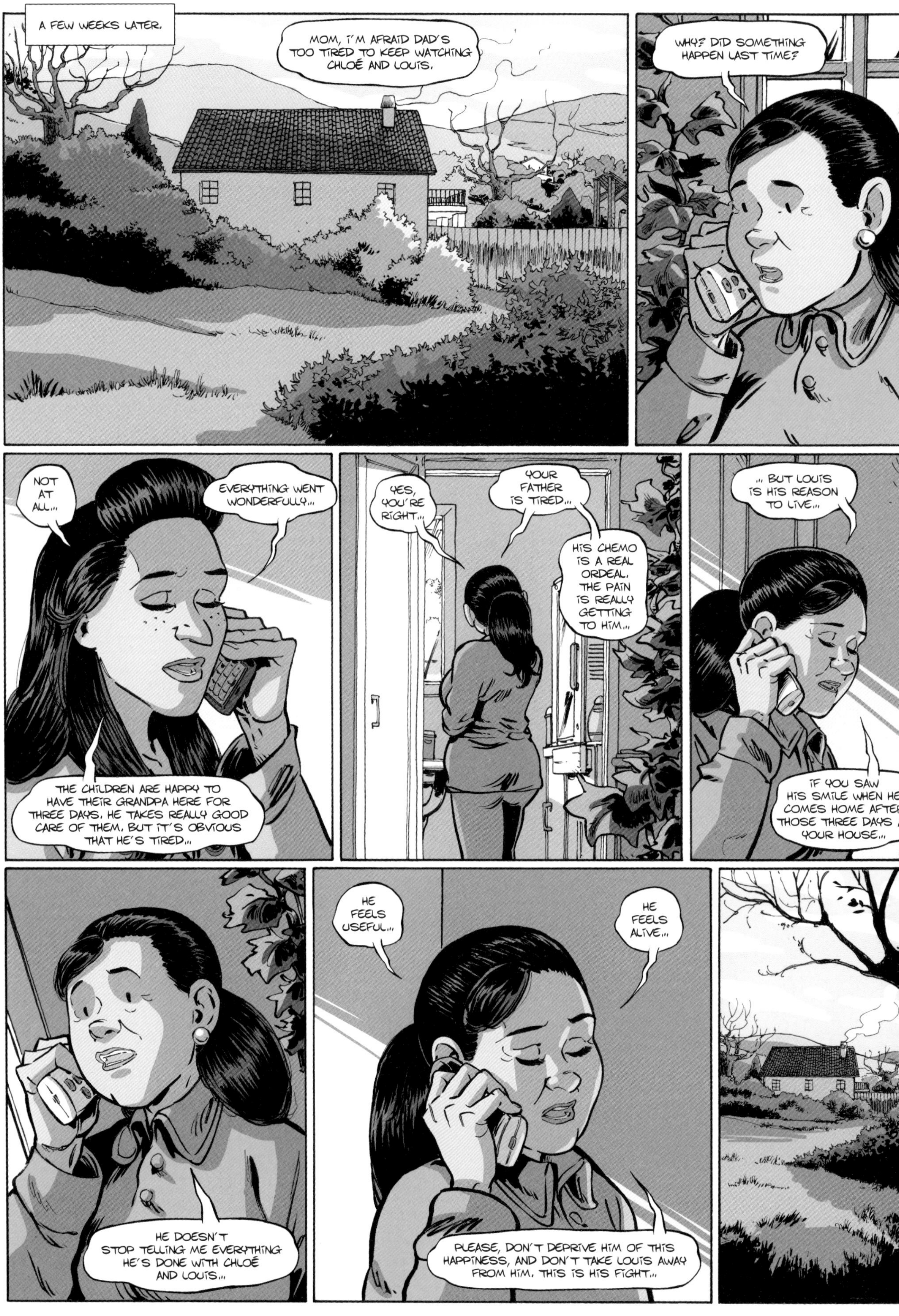
A FEW WEEKS LATER.
MOM, I'M AFRAID DAD'S TOO TIRED TO KEEP WATCHING CHLOÉ AND LOUIS.
WHY? DID SOMETHING HAPPEN LAST TIME?
NOT AT ALL...
EVERYTHING WENT WONDERFULLY...
THE CHILDREN ARE HAPPY TO HAVE THEIR GRANDPA HERE FOR THREE DAYS. HE TAKES REALLY GOOD CARE OF THEM. BUT IT'S OBVIOUS THAT HE'S TIRED...
YES, YOU'RE RIGHT...
YOUR FATHER IS TIRED...
HIS CHEMO IS A REAL ORDEAL. THE PAIN IS REALLY GETTING TO HIM...
... BUT LOUIS IS HIS REASON TO LIVE...
IF YOU SAW HIS SMILE WHEN HE COMES HOME AFTER THOSE THREE DAYS AT YOUR HOUSE...
HE DOESN'T STOP TELLING ME EVERYTHING HE'S DONE WITH CHLOÉ AND LOUIS...
HE FEELS USEFUL...
HE FEELS ALIVE...
PLEASE, DON'T DEPRIVE HIM OF THIS HAPPINESS, AND DON'T TAKE LOUIS AWAY FROM HIM. THIS IS HIS FIGHT...

SCHOOL
Ich habe keine ...
ZEIT!
CRRRR!
CRRRR

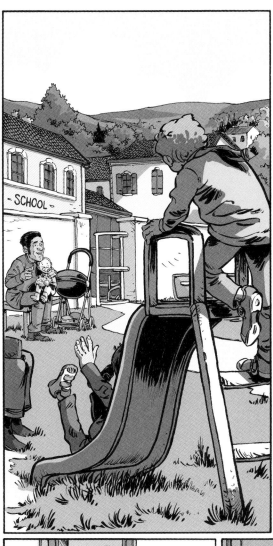

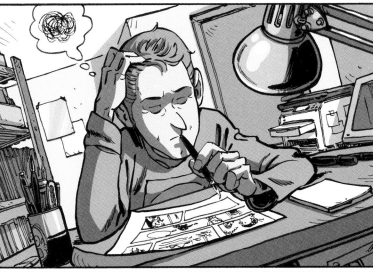

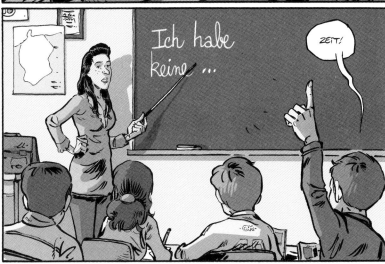

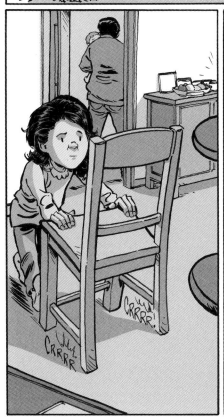

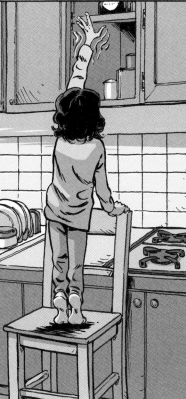

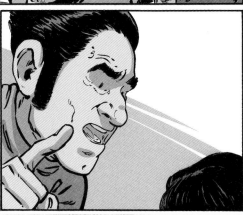

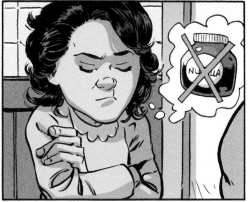

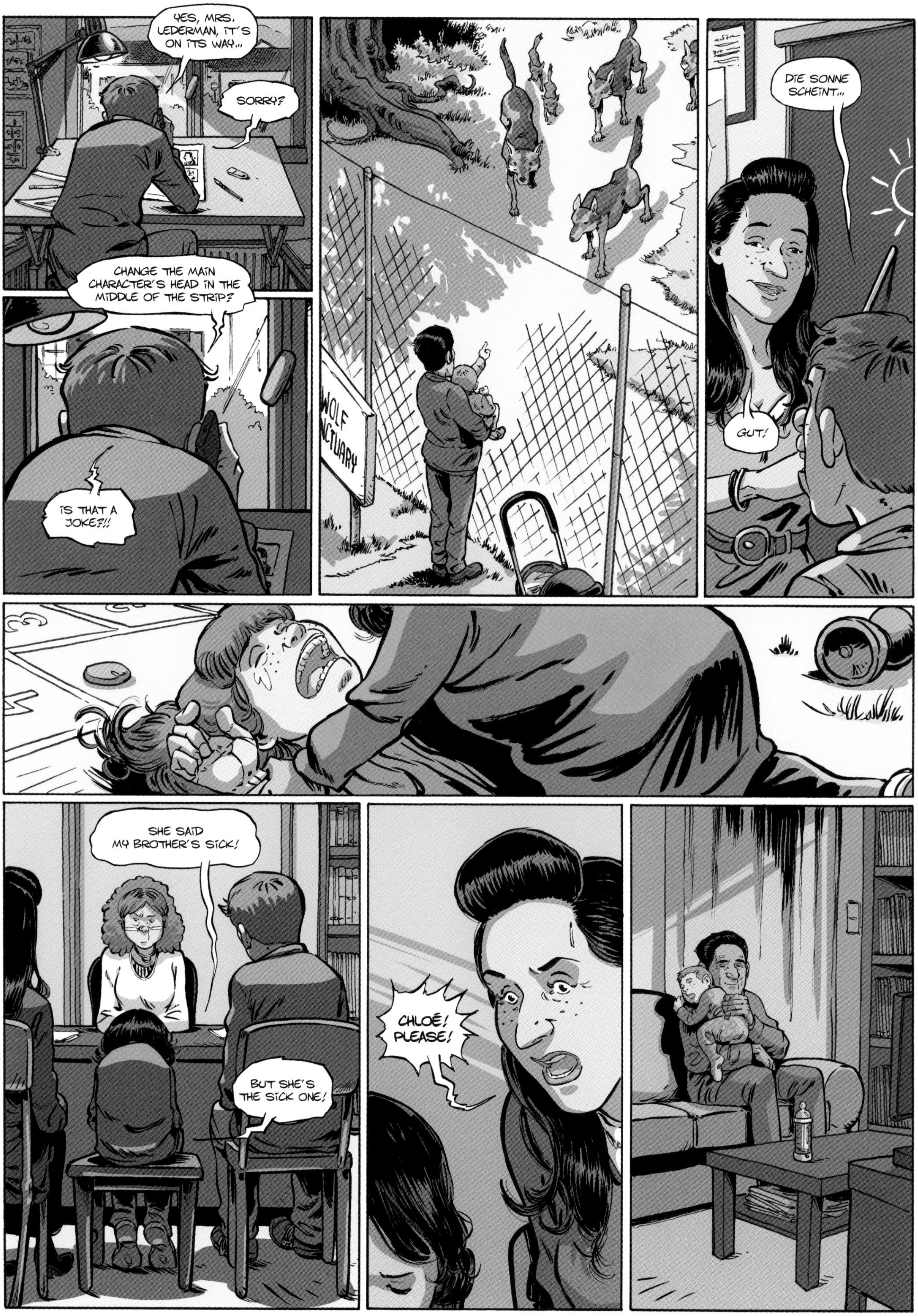
YES, MRS. LEDERMAN, IT'S ON ITS WAY...
SORRY?
CHANGE THE MAIN CHARACTER'S HEAD IN THE MIDDLE OF THE STRIP?
IS THAT A JOKE?!!
WOLF
NCTUARY
DIE SONNE SCHEINT...
GUT!
SHE SAID MY BROTHER'S SICK!
BUT SHE'S THE SICK ONE!
CHLOÉ! PLEASE!

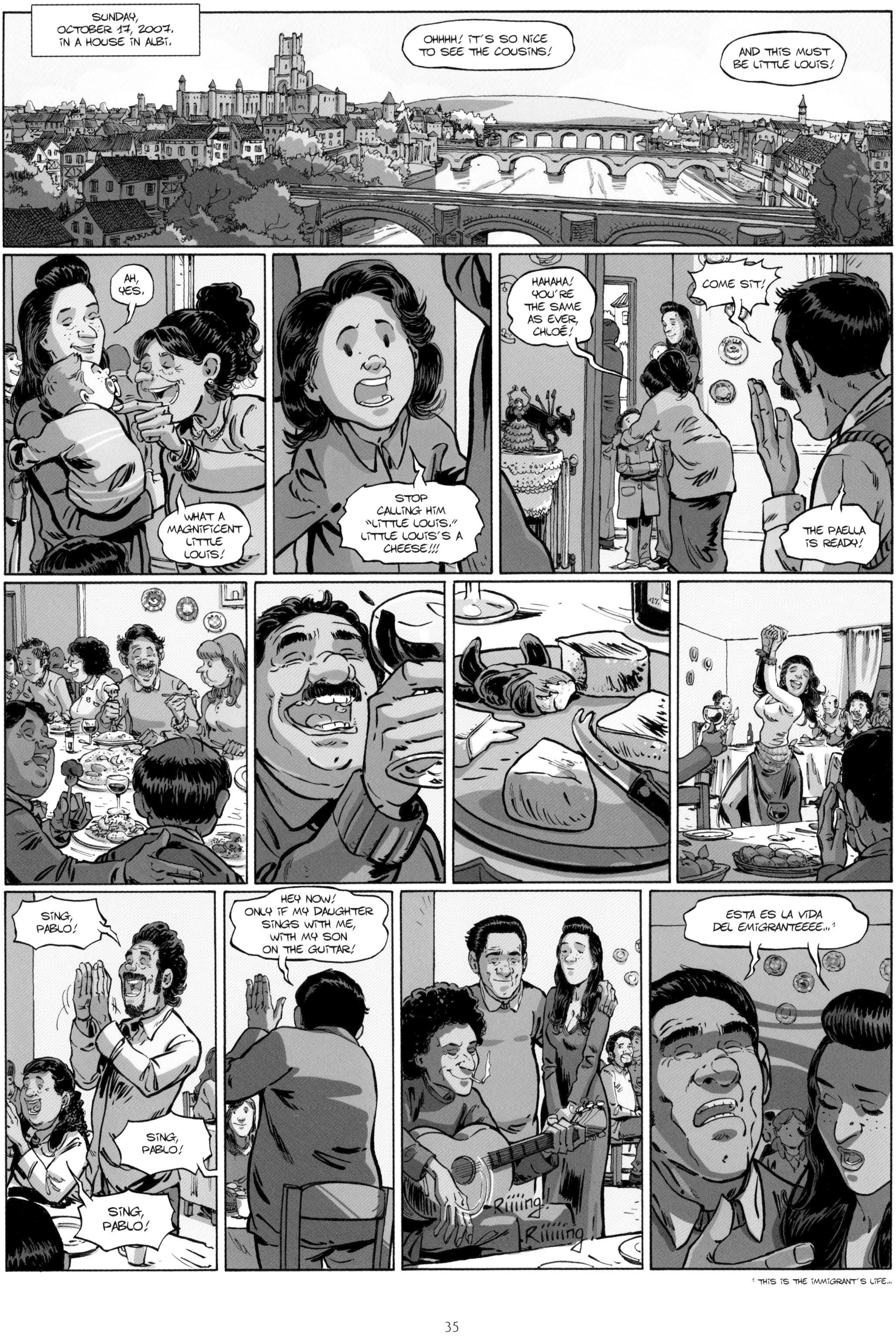
SUNDAY, OCTOBER 17, 2007, IN A HOUSE IN ALBI.
OHHHH! IT'S SO NICE TO SEE THE COUSINS!
AND THIS MUST BE LITTLE LOUIS!
AH, YES.
WHAT A MAGNIFICENT LITTLE LOUIS!
STOP CALLING HIM "LITTLE LOUIS." LITTLE LOUIS'S A CHEESE!!!
HAHAHA! YOU'RE THE SAME AS EVER, CHLOÉ!
COME SIT!
THE PAELLA IS READY!
SING, PABLO!
SING, PABLO!
SING, PABLO!
HEY NOW! ONLY IF MY DAUGHTER SINGS WITH ME, WITH MY SON ON THE GUITAR!
Riiiing
Riiiing
ESTA ES LA VIDA DEL EMIGRANTEEEE...[1]

[1] THIS IS THE IMMIGRANT'S LIFE...

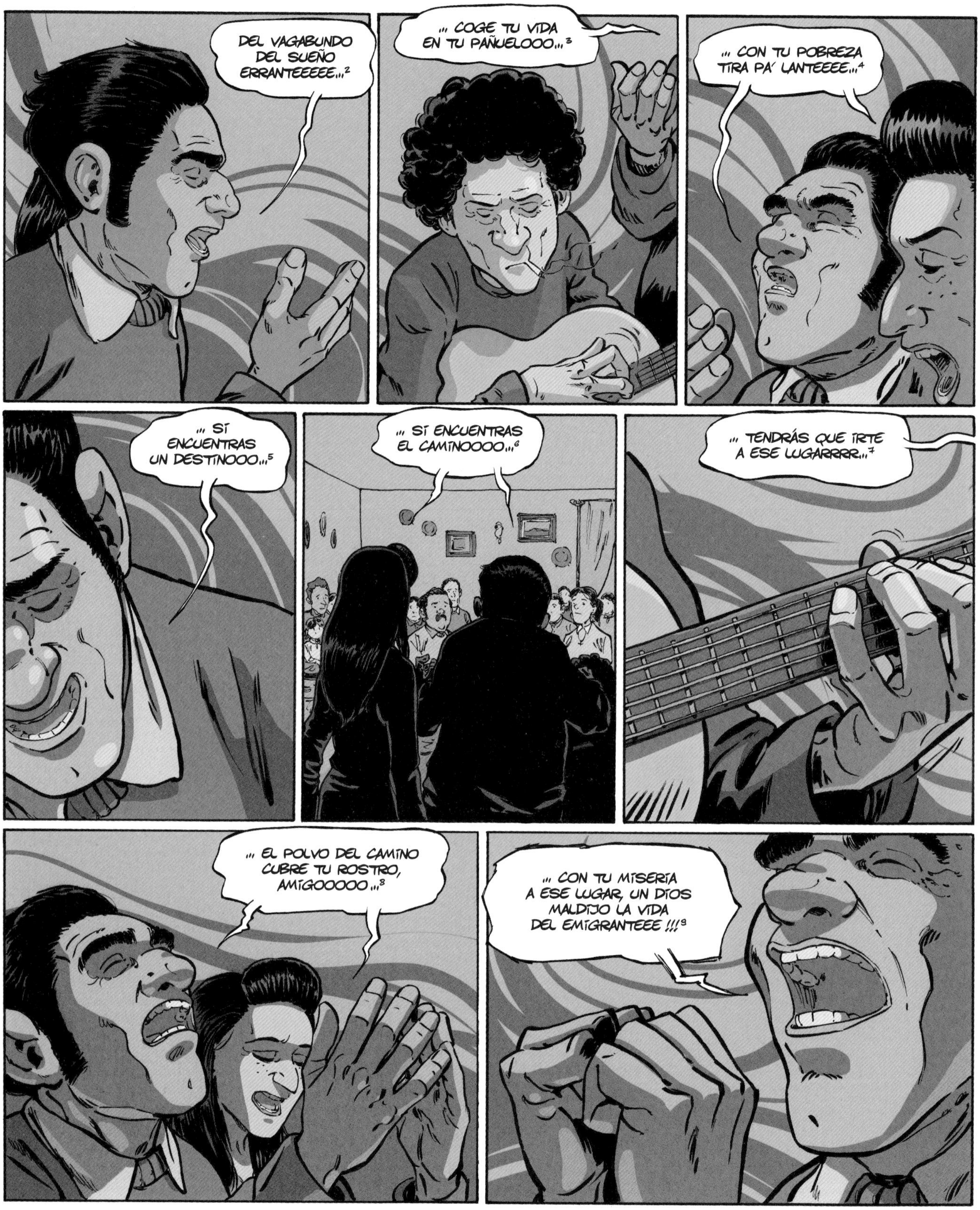
DEL VAGABUNDO DEL SUEÑO ERRANTEEEEE...[2]
... COGE TU VIDA EN TU PAÑUELOOO...[3]
... CON TU POBREZA TIRA PA' LANTEEEE...[4]
... SI ENCUENTRAS UN DESTINOOO...[5]
... SI ENCUENTRAS EL CAMINOOOO...[6]
... TENDRÁS QUE IRTE A ESE LUGARRRR...[7]
... EL POLVO DEL CAMINO CUBRE TU ROSTRO, AMIGOOOOO...[8]
... CON TU MISERIA A ESE LUGAR, UN DIOS MALDIJO LA VIDA DEL EMIGRANTEEE !!![9]

[2] OF THE VAGABOND AND HIS WANDERING DREAM...

[3] PACK YOUR LIFE IN YOUR BUNDLE...

[4] WITH YOUR POVERTY FORGE ONWARD...

[5] IF YOU FIND FORTUNE...

[6] IF YOU FIND THE PATH...

[7] YOU MUST GO TO THAT PLACE...

[8] THE DUST OF THE ROAD WILL COVER YOUR FACE, FRIEND...

[9] WHEN THAT PLACE FILLS YOU WITH WOE, A GOD CURSES THE IMMIGRANT'S LIFE!!!

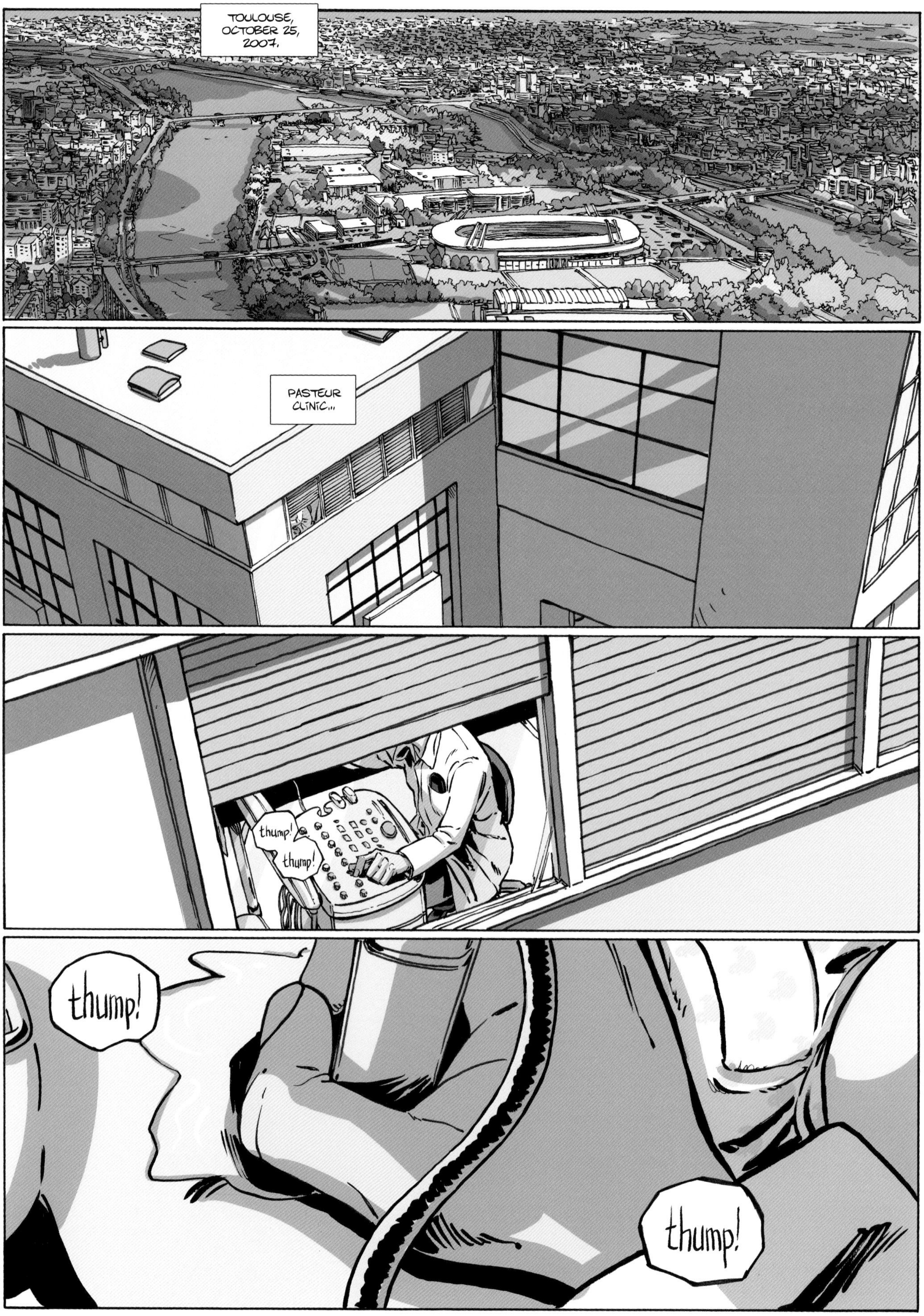
TOULOUSE, OCTOBER 25, 2007.
PASTEUR CLINIC...
thump!
thump!
thump!
thump!

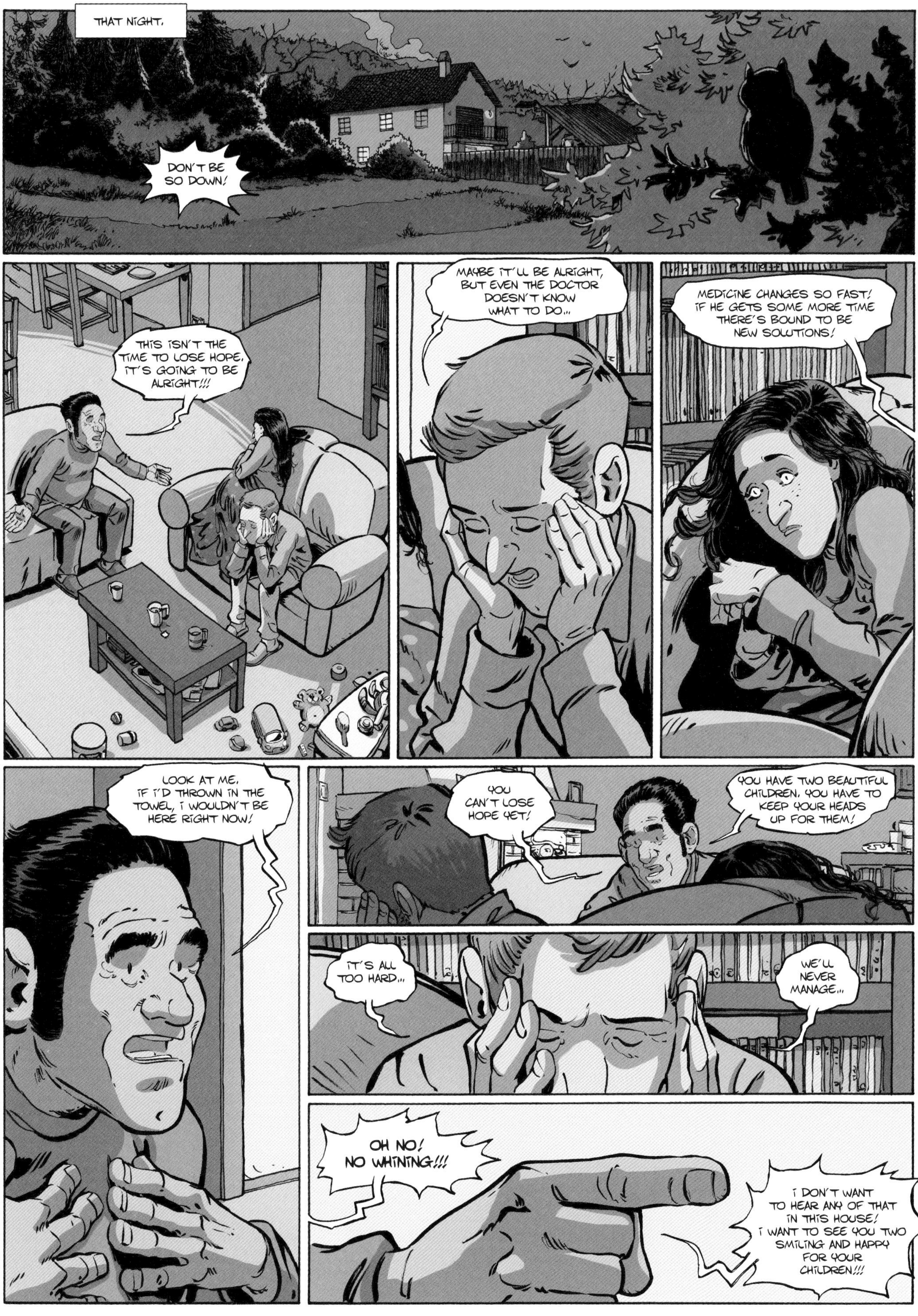
THAT NIGHT.
DON'T BE SO DOWN!
THIS ISN'T THE TIME TO LOSE HOPE. IT'S GOING TO BE ALRIGHT!!!
MAYBE IT'LL BE ALRIGHT, BUT EVEN THE DOCTOR DOESN'T KNOW WHAT TO DO...
MEDICINE CHANGES SO FAST! IF HE GETS SOME MORE TIME THERE'S BOUND TO BE NEW SOLUTIONS!
LOOK AT ME. IF I'D THROWN IN THE TOWEL, I WOULDN'T BE HERE RIGHT NOW!
YOU CAN'T LOSE HOPE YET!
YOU HAVE TWO BEAUTIFUL CHILDREN. YOU HAVE TO KEEP YOUR HEADS UP FOR THEM!
IT'S ALL TOO HARD...
WE'LL NEVER MANAGE...
OH NO! NO WHINING!!!
I DON'T WANT TO HEAR ANY OF THAT IN THIS HOUSE! I WANT TO SEE YOU TWO SMILING AND HAPPY FOR YOUR CHILDREN!!!

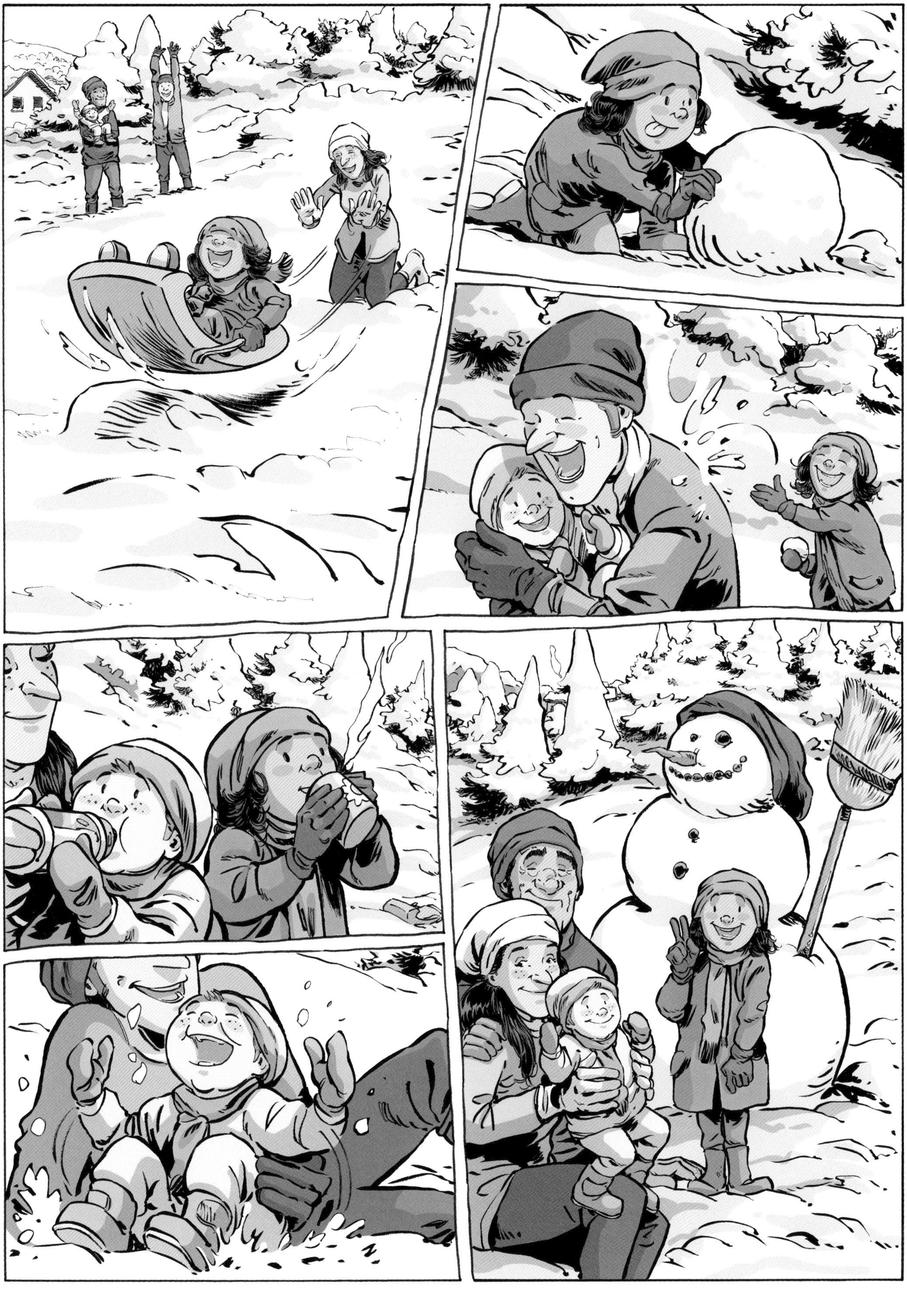

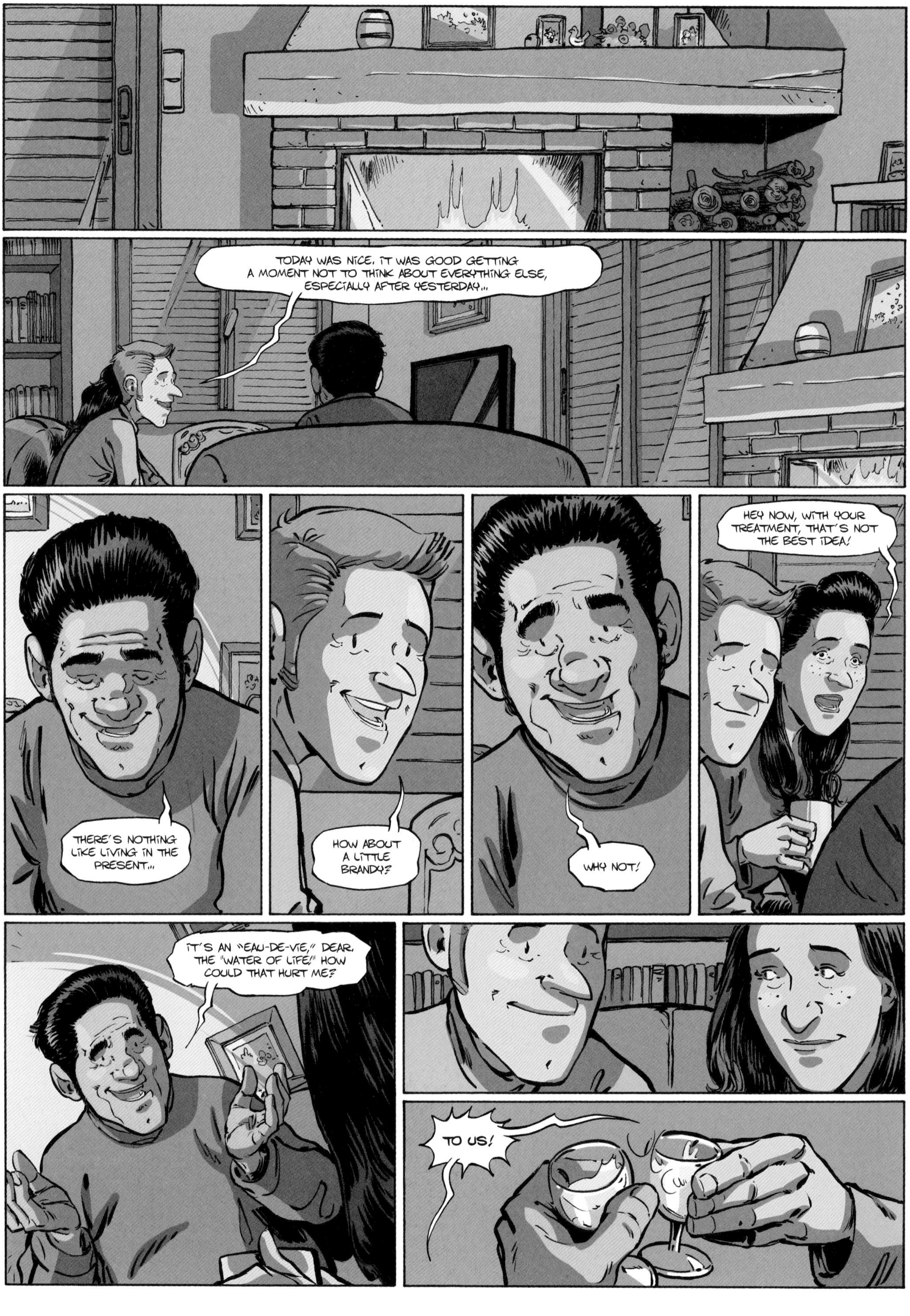
TODAY WAS NICE. IT WAS GOOD GETTING A MOMENT NOT TO THINK ABOUT EVERYTHING ELSE, ESPECIALLY AFTER YESTERDAY...
THERE'S NOTHING LIKE LIVING IN THE PRESENT...
HOW ABOUT A LITTLE BRANDY?
WHY NOT!
HEY NOW, WITH YOUR TREATMENT, THAT'S NOT THE BEST IDEA!
IT'S AN "EAU-DE-VIE," DEAR. THE "WATER OF LIFE!" HOW COULD THAT HURT ME?
TO US!

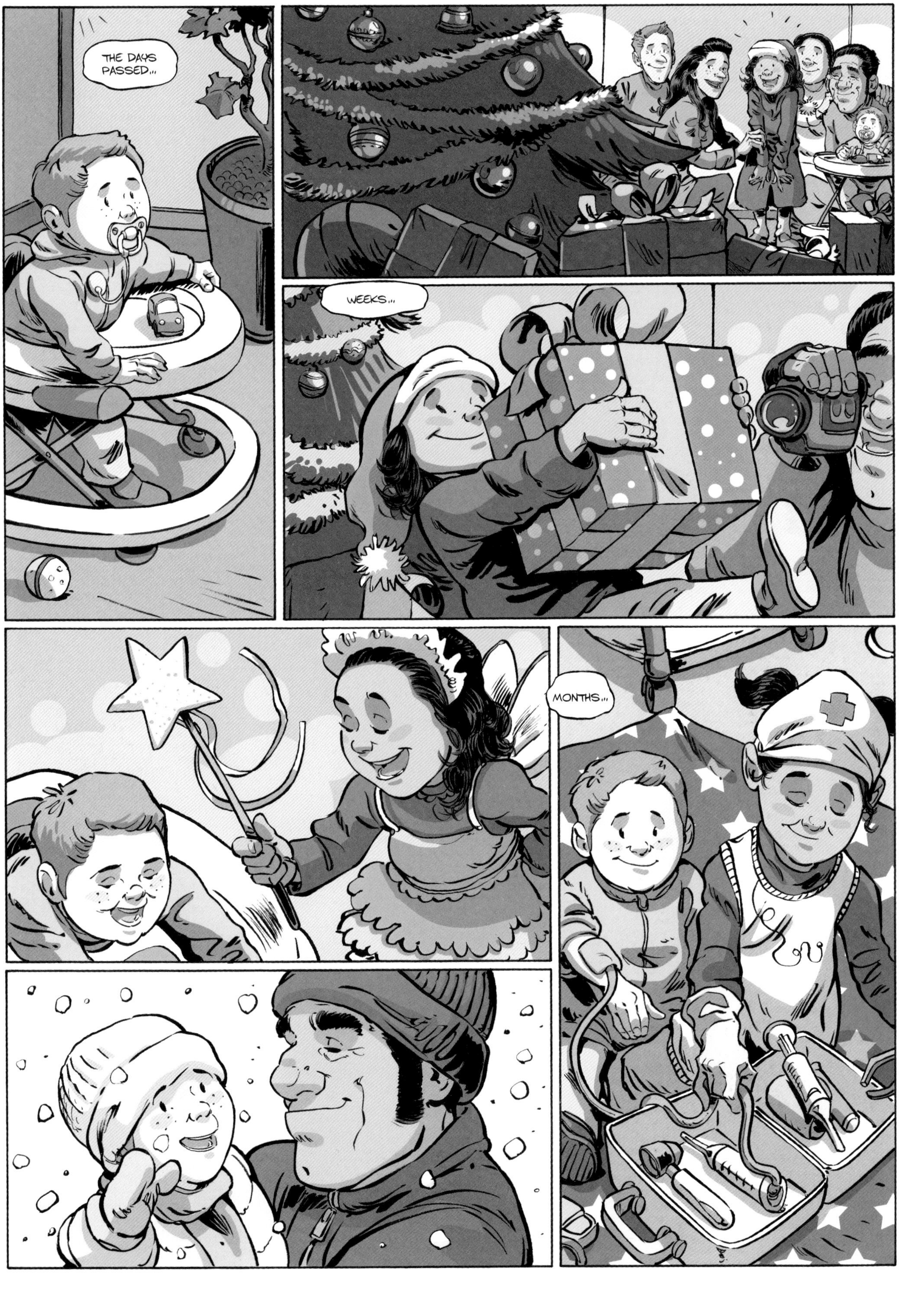
THE DAYS PASSED...
WEEKS...
MONTHS...

46

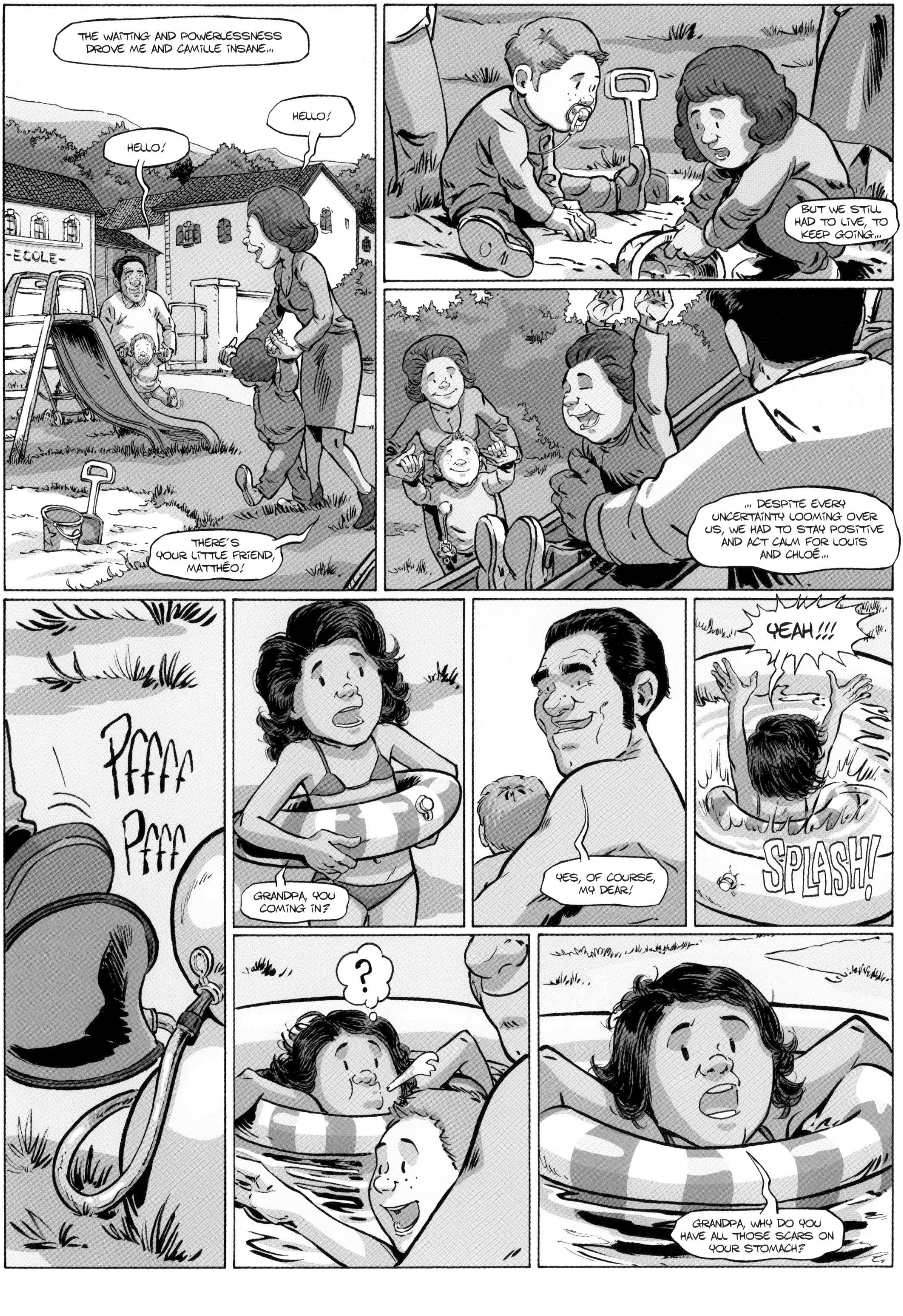

THE WAITING AND POWERLESSNESS DROVE ME AND CAMILLE INSANE...
HELLO!
HELLO!
-ECOLE-
THERE'S YOUR LITTLE FRIEND, MATTHÉO!
BUT WE STILL HAD TO LIVE, TO KEEP GOING...
... DESPITE EVERY UNCERTAINTY LOOMING OVER US, WE HAD TO STAY POSITIVE AND ACT CALM FOR LOUIS AND CHLOÉ...
Pffff
Pfff
GRANDPA, YOU COMING IN?
YES, OF COURSE, MY DEAR!
YEAH!!!
SPLASH!
?
GRANDPA, WHY DO YOU HAVE ALL THOSE SCARS ON YOUR STOMACH?

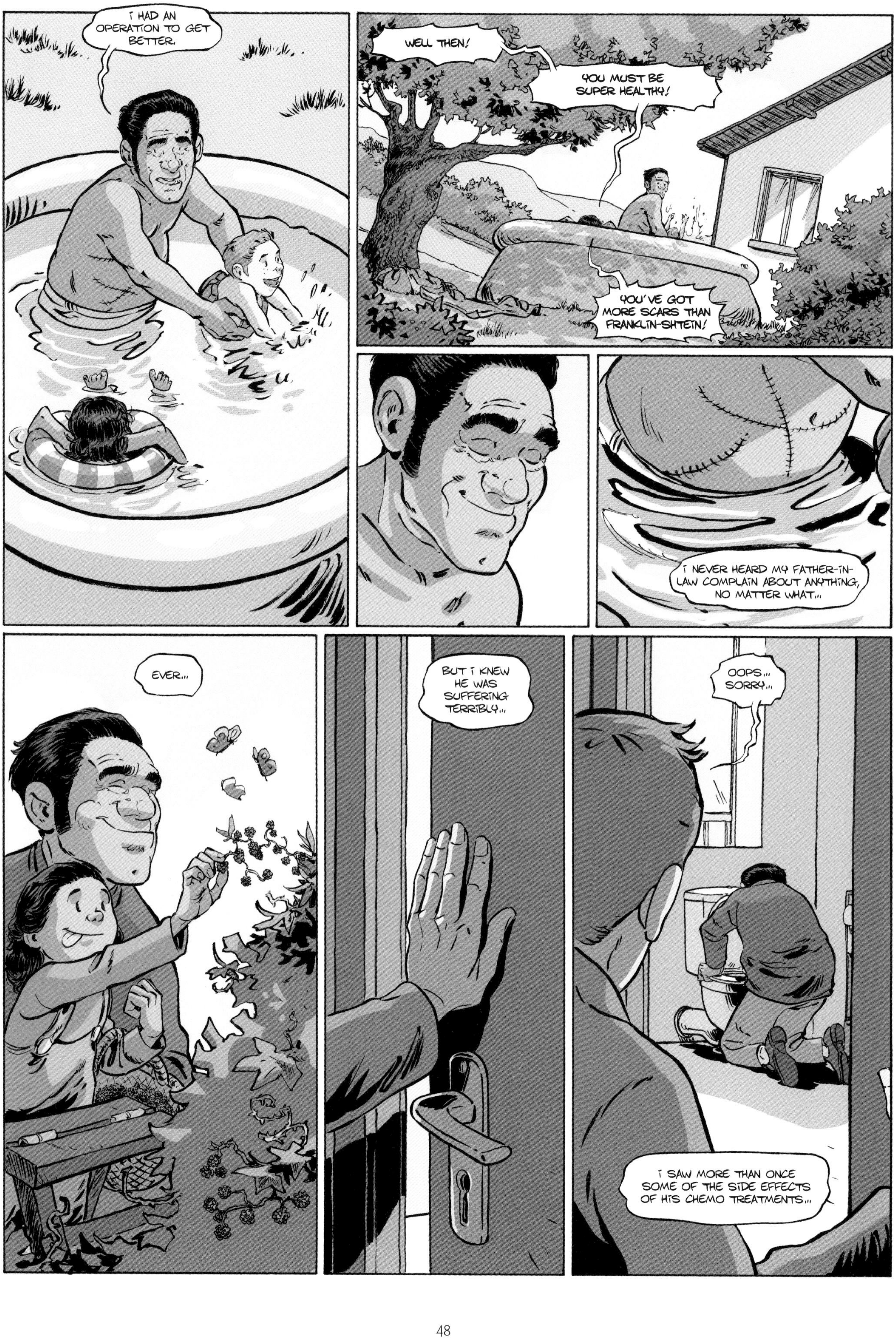
I HAD AN OPERATION TO GET BETTER.
WELL THEN!
YOU MUST BE SUPER HEALTHY!
YOU'VE GOT MORE SCARS THAN FRANKLIN-SHTEIN!
I NEVER HEARD MY FATHER-IN-LAW COMPLAIN ABOUT ANYTHING, NO MATTER WHAT...
EVER...
BUT I KNEW HE WAS SUFFERING TERRIBLY...
OOPS... SORRY...
I SAW MORE THAN ONCE SOME OF THE SIDE EFFECTS OF HIS CHEMO TREATMENTS...

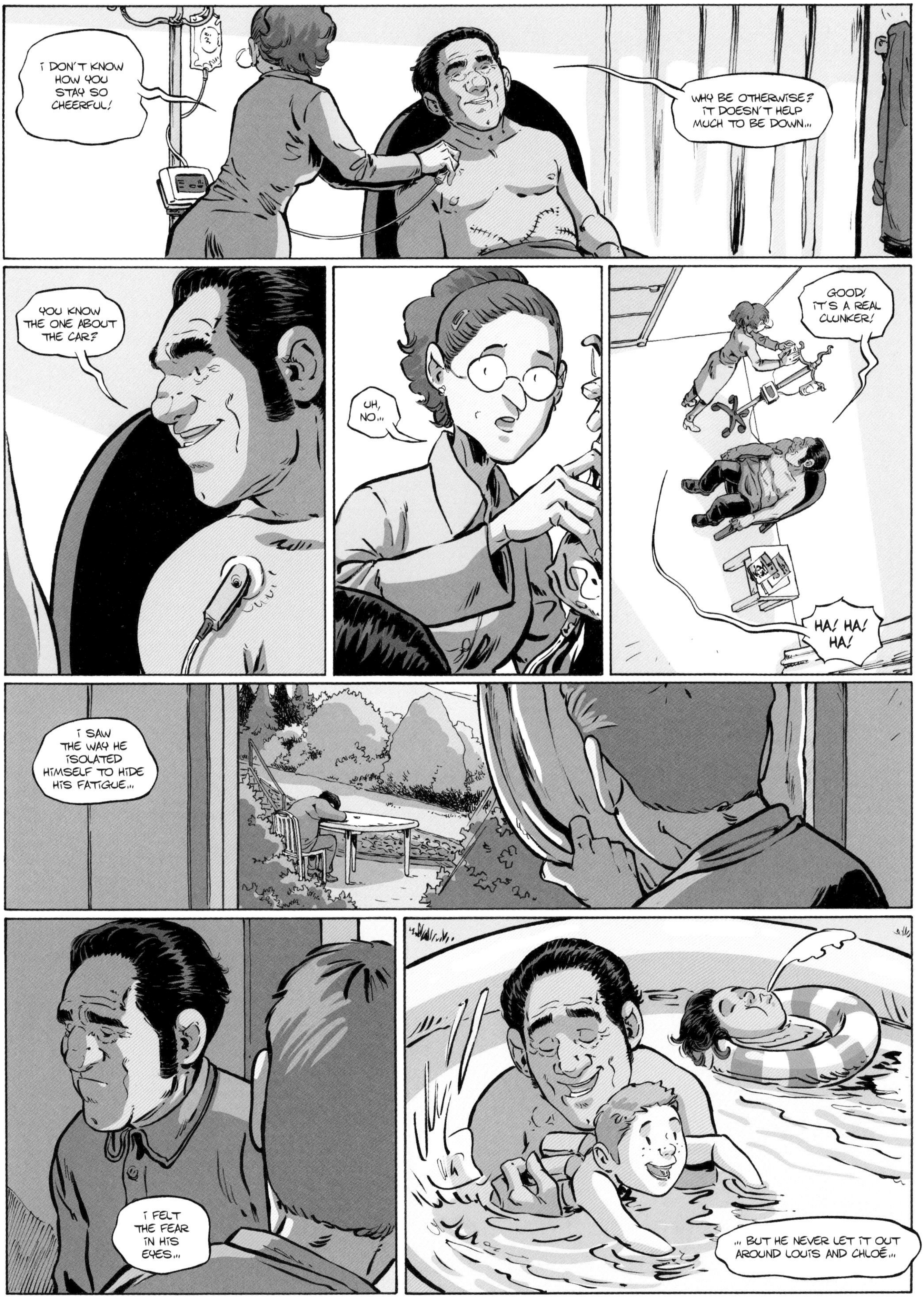
I DON'T KNOW HOW YOU STAY SO CHEERFUL!
WHY BE OTHERWISE? IT DOESN'T HELP MUCH TO BE DOWN...
YOU KNOW THE ONE ABOUT THE CAR?
UH, NO...
GOOD! IT'S A REAL CLUNKER!
HA! HA! HA!
I SAW THE WAY HE ISOLATED HIMSELF TO HIDE HIS FATIGUE...
I FELT THE FEAR IN HIS EYES...
... BUT HE NEVER LET IT OUT AROUND LOUIS AND CHLOÉ...

50

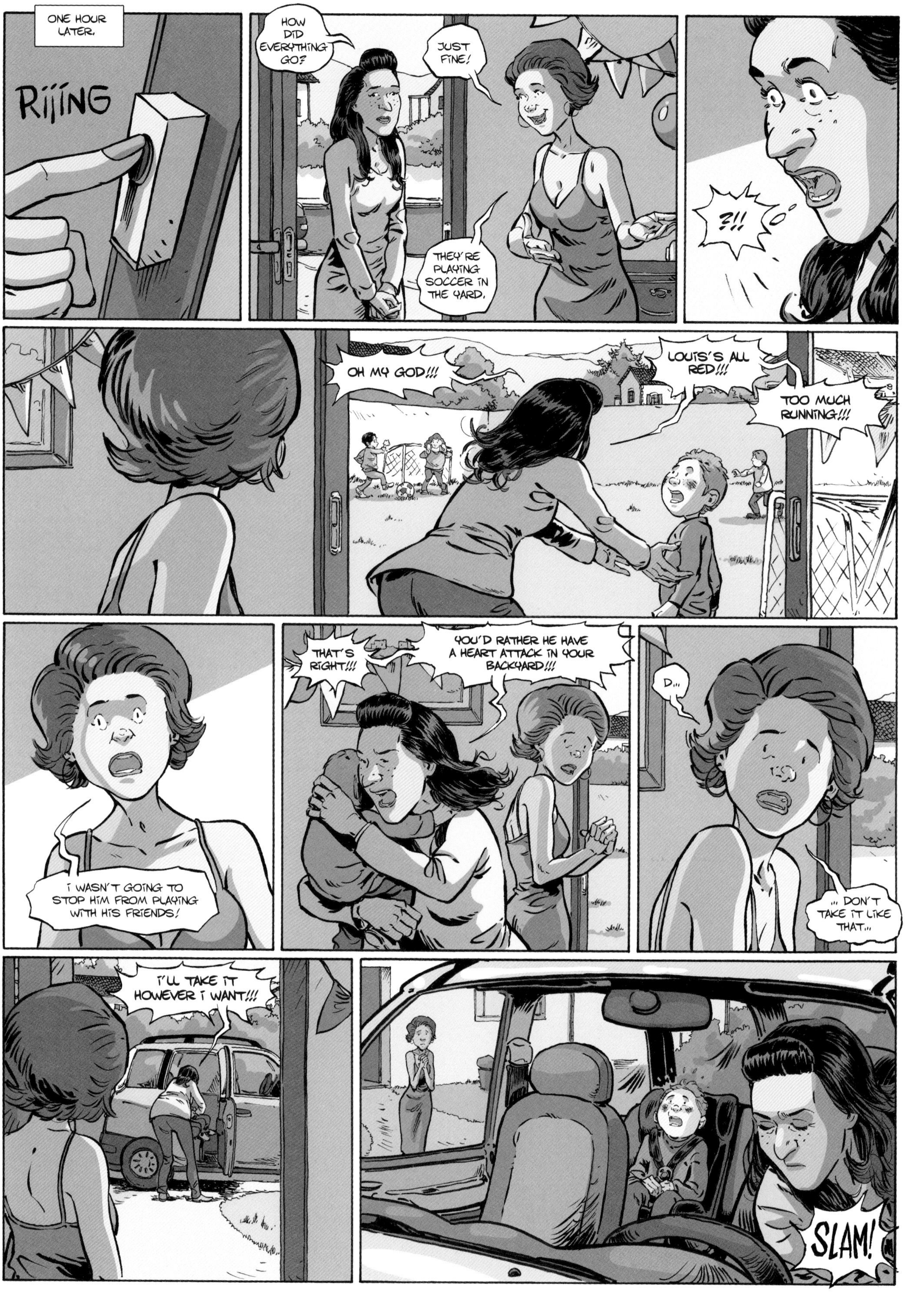
ONE HOUR LATER.
RIIING
HOW DID EVERYTHING GO?
JUST FINE!
THEY'RE PLAYING SOCCER IN THE YARD.
?!!
OH MY GOD!!!
LOUIS'S ALL RED!!!
TOO MUCH RUNNING!!!
I WASN'T GOING TO STOP HIM FROM PLAYING WITH HIS FRIENDS!
THAT'S RIGHT!!!
YOU'D RATHER HE HAVE A HEART ATTACK IN YOUR BACKYARD!!!
D...
... DON'T TAKE IT LIKE THAT...
I'LL TAKE IT HOWEVER I WANT!!!
SLAM!

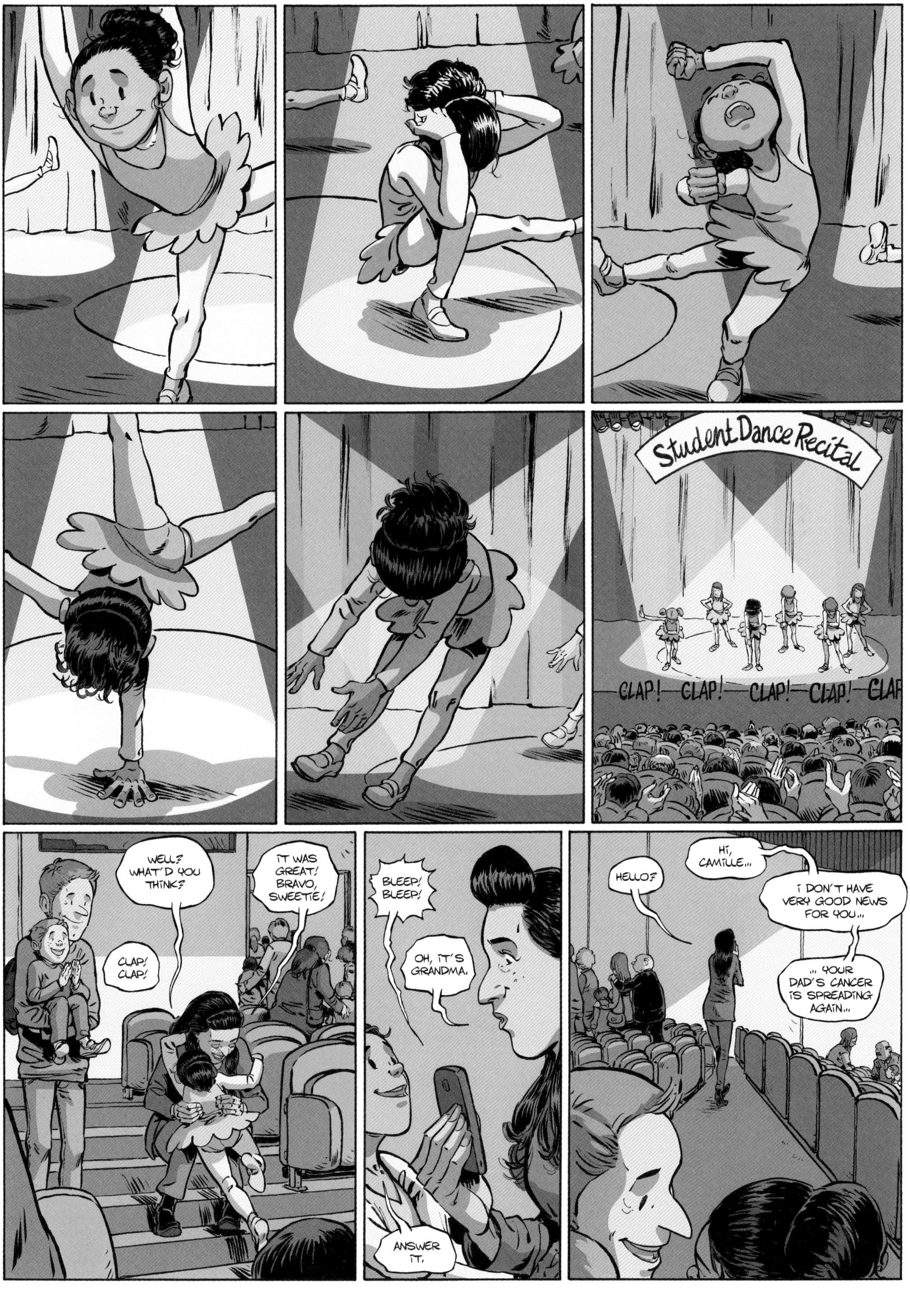
Student Dance Recital
CLAP! CLAP! CLAP! CLAP! CLAP
WELL? WHAT'D YOU THINK?
CLAP! CLAP!
IT WAS GREAT! BRAVO, SWEETIE!
BLEEP! BLEEP!
OH, IT'S GRANDMA.
ANSWER IT.
HELLO?
HI, CAMILLE...
I DON'T HAVE VERY GOOD NEWS FOR YOU...
... YOUR DAD'S CANCER IS SPREADING AGAIN...

THE NEXT DAY.

WHOA, YOU'RE BREAKING OUT THE OLD STUFF!

YES...

I WANT TO TRY GOING ON A RIDE WITH SOME FRIENDS THIS AFTERNOON IN VARILHES.

EXCELLENT IDEA! I'M GOING TO SEE A CARTOON AT THE THEATER IN PAMIERS WITH LOUIS AND CHLOÉ.

YOU WON'T HAVE TO BE ALL ALONE NOW SINCE YOU HATE MOVIES SO MUCH...

BLAH BLAH BLAH...

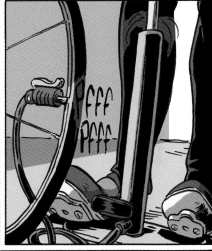

PFFF PFFF

WILL YOU TAKE ME ON A BIKE RIDE ONE DAY, DAD?

OF COURSE, LOUIS, WE'LL GO RIDING TOGETHER WHEN YOU'RE OLDER!

BUT SLOWLY, RIGHT?

... WITH MY HEART PROBLEMS, I CAN'T GO FAST...

I KNOW, MY TREASURE... I KNOW...

55

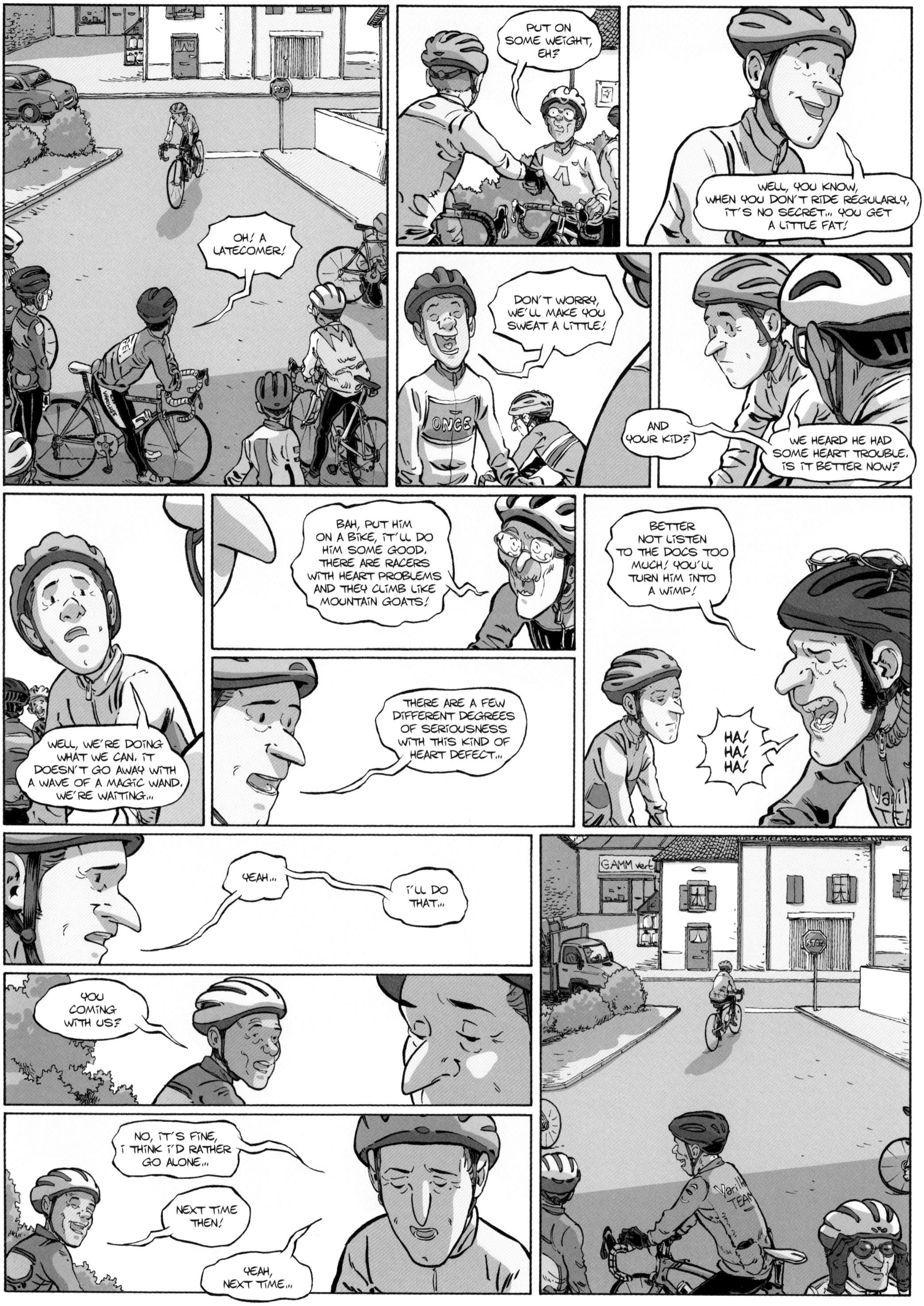
STOP
OH! A LATECOMER!
PUT ON SOME WEIGHT, EH?
WELL, YOU KNOW, WHEN YOU DON'T RIDE REGULARLY, IT'S NO SECRET... YOU GET A LITTLE FAT!
DON'T WORRY, WE'LL MAKE YOU SWEAT A LITTLE!
ONGE
AND YOUR KID?
WE HEARD HE HAD SOME HEART TROUBLE. IS IT BETTER NOW?
WELL, WE'RE DOING WHAT WE CAN. IT DOESN'T GO AWAY WITH A WAVE OF A MAGIC WAND. WE'RE WAITING...
BAH, PUT HIM ON A BIKE, IT'LL DO HIM SOME GOOD. THERE ARE RACERS WITH HEART PROBLEMS AND THEY CLIMB LIKE MOUNTAIN GOATS!
THERE ARE A FEW DIFFERENT DEGREES OF SERIOUSNESS WITH THIS KIND OF HEART DEFECT...
BETTER NOT LISTEN TO THE DOCS TOO MUCH! YOU'LL TURN HIM INTO A WIMP!
HA! HA! HA!
YEAH...
I'LL DO THAT...
YOU COMING WITH US?
NO, IT'S FINE, I THINK I'D RATHER GO ALONE...
NEXT TIME THEN!
YEAH, NEXT TIME...
GAMM vert
STOP

57

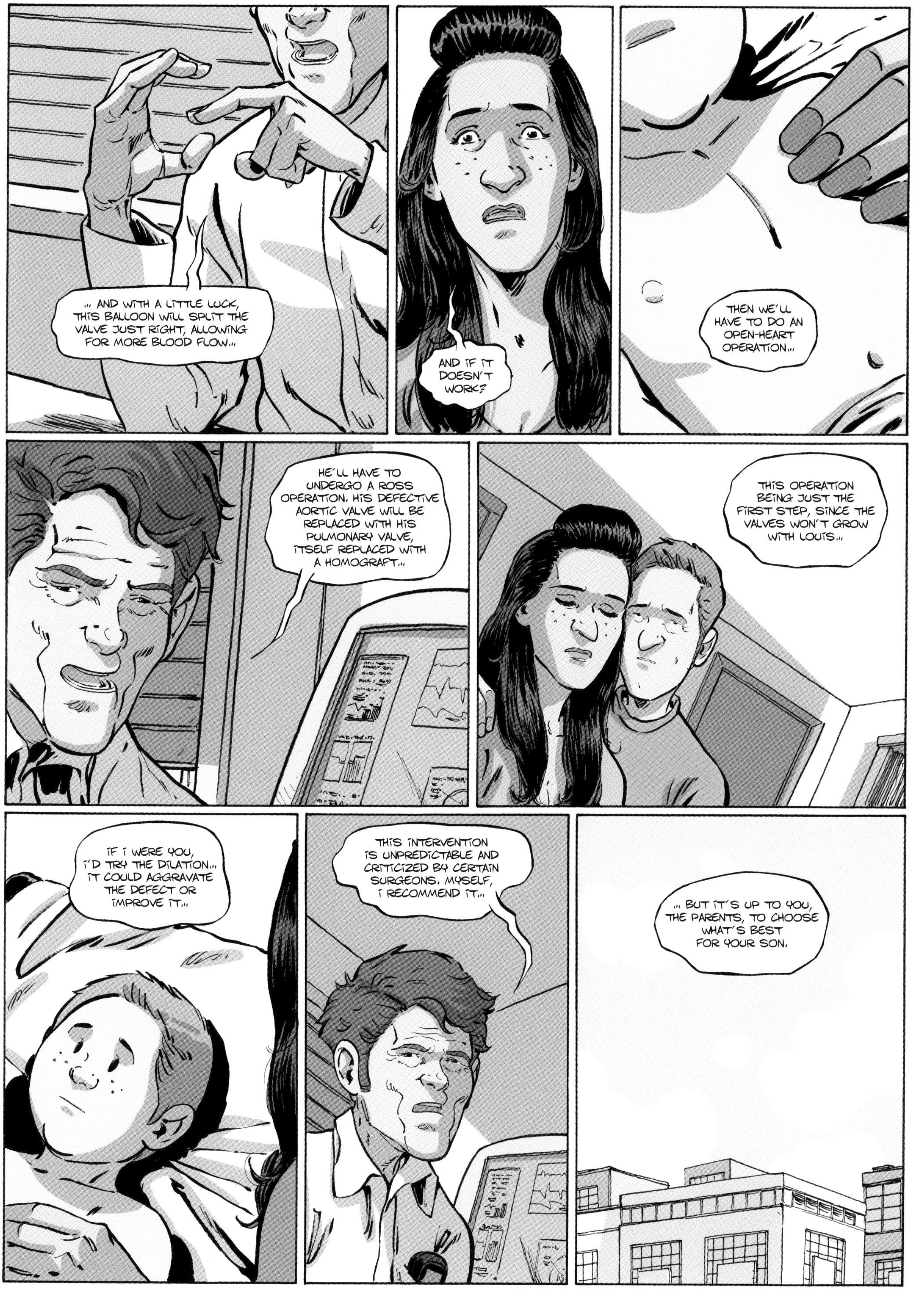
... AND WITH A LITTLE LUCK, THIS BALLOON WILL SPLIT THE VALVE JUST RIGHT, ALLOWING FOR MORE BLOOD FLOW...
AND IF IT DOESN'T WORK?
THEN WE'LL HAVE TO DO AN OPEN-HEART OPERATION...
HE'LL HAVE TO UNDERGO A ROSS OPERATION. HIS DEFECTIVE AORTIC VALVE WILL BE REPLACED WITH HIS PULMONARY VALVE, ITSELF REPLACED WITH A HOMOGRAFT...
THIS OPERATION BEING JUST THE FIRST STEP, SINCE THE VALVES WON'T GROW WITH LOUIS...
IF I WERE YOU, I'D TRY THE DILATION... IT COULD AGGRAVATE THE DEFECT OR IMPROVE IT...
THIS INTERVENTION IS UNPREDICTABLE AND CRITICIZED BY CERTAIN SURGEONS. MYSELF, I RECOMMEND IT...
... BUT IT'S UP TO YOU, THE PARENTS, TO CHOOSE WHAT'S BEST FOR YOUR SON.

BONK!

DO YOU REMEMBER THE FIRST TIME I SAW YOU WITH MY SISTER?

ARE YOU KIDDING? HOW COULD I FORGET?!

DO TELL!

WE WERE FIFTEEN, AND CAMILLE AND I HAD JUST STARTED GOING OUT TOGETHER...

WE WERE WITH FRIENDS AT A CAFÉ IN MAZAMET, BY THE WINDOW.

SCREEEECH!!

A RENAULT 5 PULLED UP IN FRONT OF THE CAFÉ, TWO GUYS GOT OUT, ONE TALL AND ONE SHORT, DRESSED LIKE HARD ROCKERS...

THE TALL ONE WAS YOUR COUSIN, ALBERTO, THE SHORT ONE WAS A FRIEND OF HIS...

YOU, THERE!!! YOU BETTER NOT HURT MY SISTER!!!

GOT IT?!

WHAM

THEY CAME INTO THE CAFÉ LIKE TWO FURIES...

ALBERTO STOMPED UP TO ME AND SAID...

AND THEN THEY IMMEDIATELY LEFT.

WHAM!

AHA! AND SO, TWENTY YEARS LATER, YOU'RE STILL WITH HER!

YOU WERE SO SHOCKED! HAHA!

HA HA HA HA!

THROW, MORON!

64

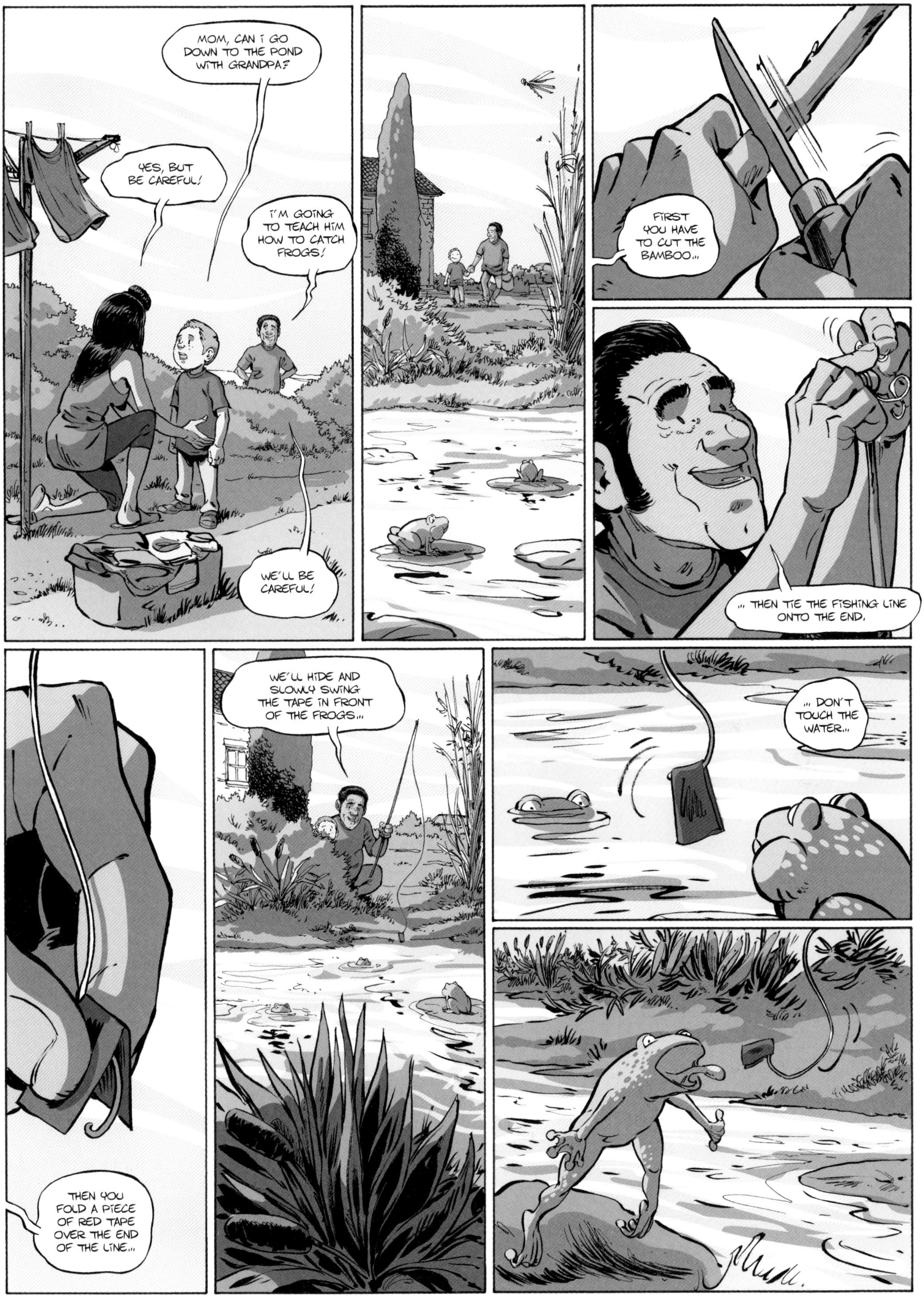
MOM, CAN I GO DOWN TO THE POND WITH GRANDPA?
YES, BUT BE CAREFUL!
I'M GOING TO TEACH HIM HOW TO CATCH FROGS!
WE'LL BE CAREFUL!
FIRST YOU HAVE TO CUT THE BAMBOO...
... THEN TIE THE FISHING LINE ONTO THE END.
THEN YOU FOLD A PIECE OF RED TAPE OVER THE END OF THE LINE...
WE'LL HIDE AND SLOWLY SWING THE TAPE IN FRONT OF THE FROGS...
... DON'T TOUCH THE WATER...

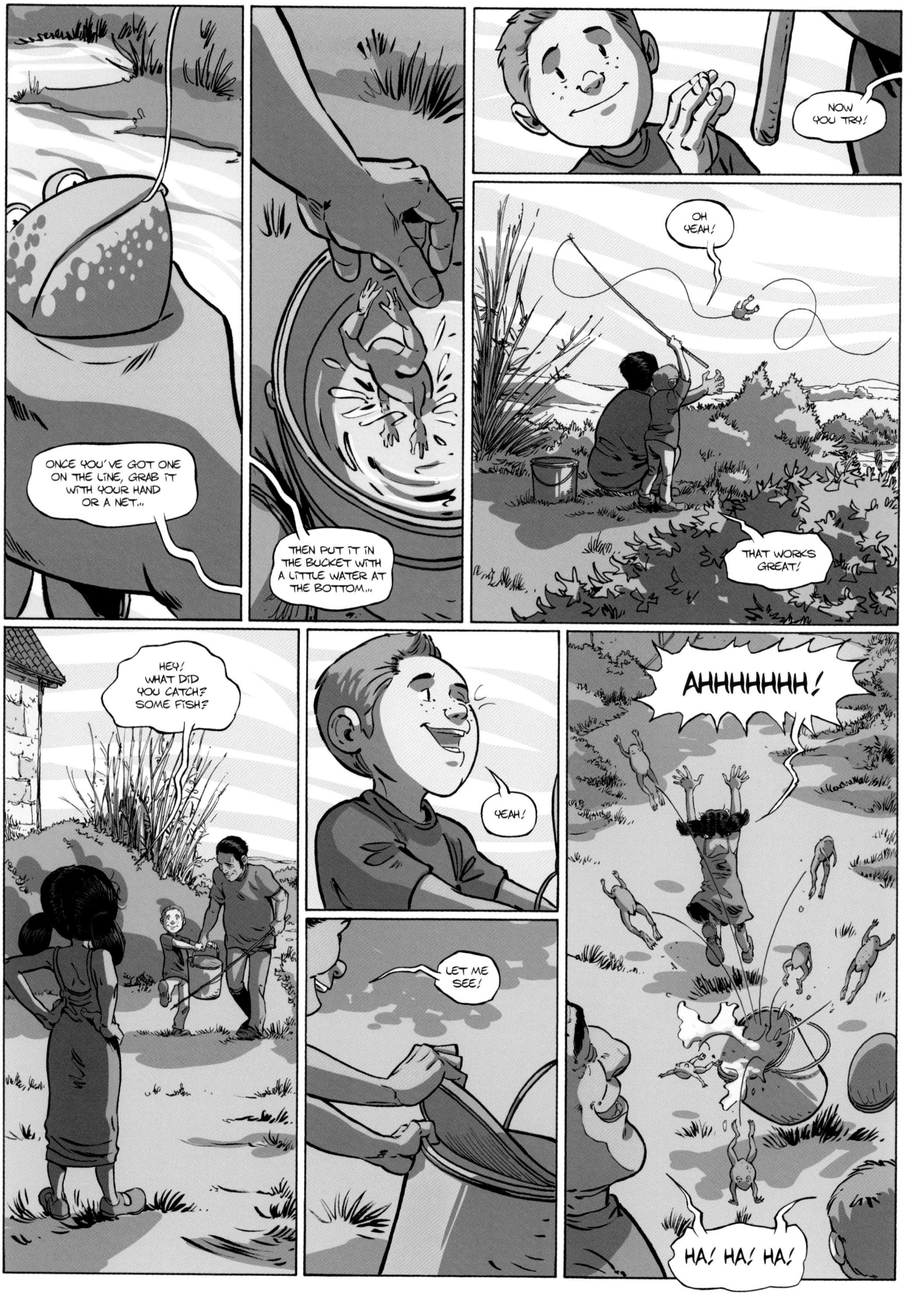
ONCE YOU'VE GOT ONE ON THE LINE, GRAB IT WITH YOUR HAND OR A NET...
THEN PUT IT IN THE BUCKET WITH A LITTLE WATER AT THE BOTTOM...
NOW YOU TRY!
OH YEAH!
THAT WORKS GREAT!
HEY! WHAT DID YOU CATCH? SOME FISH?
YEAH!
LET ME SEE!
AHHHHHHH!
HA! HA! HA!

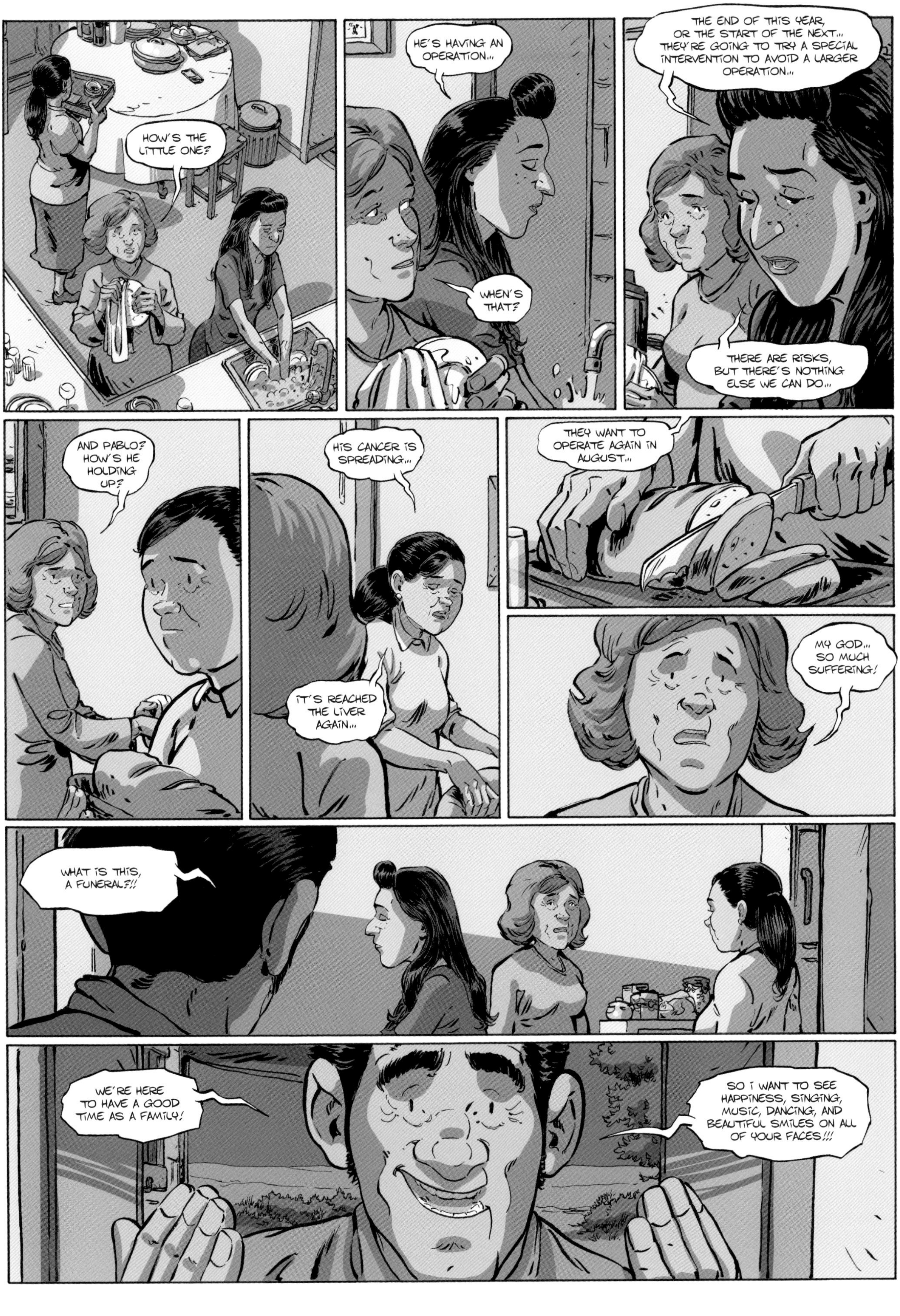
HOW'S THE LITTLE ONE?
HE'S HAVING AN OPERATION...
WHEN'S THAT?
THE END OF THIS YEAR, OR THE START OF THE NEXT... THEY'RE GOING TO TRY A SPECIAL INTERVENTION TO AVOID A LARGER OPERATION...
THERE ARE RISKS, BUT THERE'S NOTHING ELSE WE CAN DO...
AND PABLO? HOW'S HE HOLDING UP?
HIS CANCER IS SPREADING...
IT'S REACHED THE LIVER AGAIN...
THEY WANT TO OPERATE AGAIN IN AUGUST...
MY GOD... SO MUCH SUFFERING!
WHAT IS THIS, A FUNERAL?!!
WE'RE HERE TO HAVE A GOOD TIME AS A FAMILY!
SO I WANT TO SEE HAPPINESS, SINGING, MUSIC, DANCING, AND BEAUTIFUL SMILES ON ALL OF YOUR FACES!!!

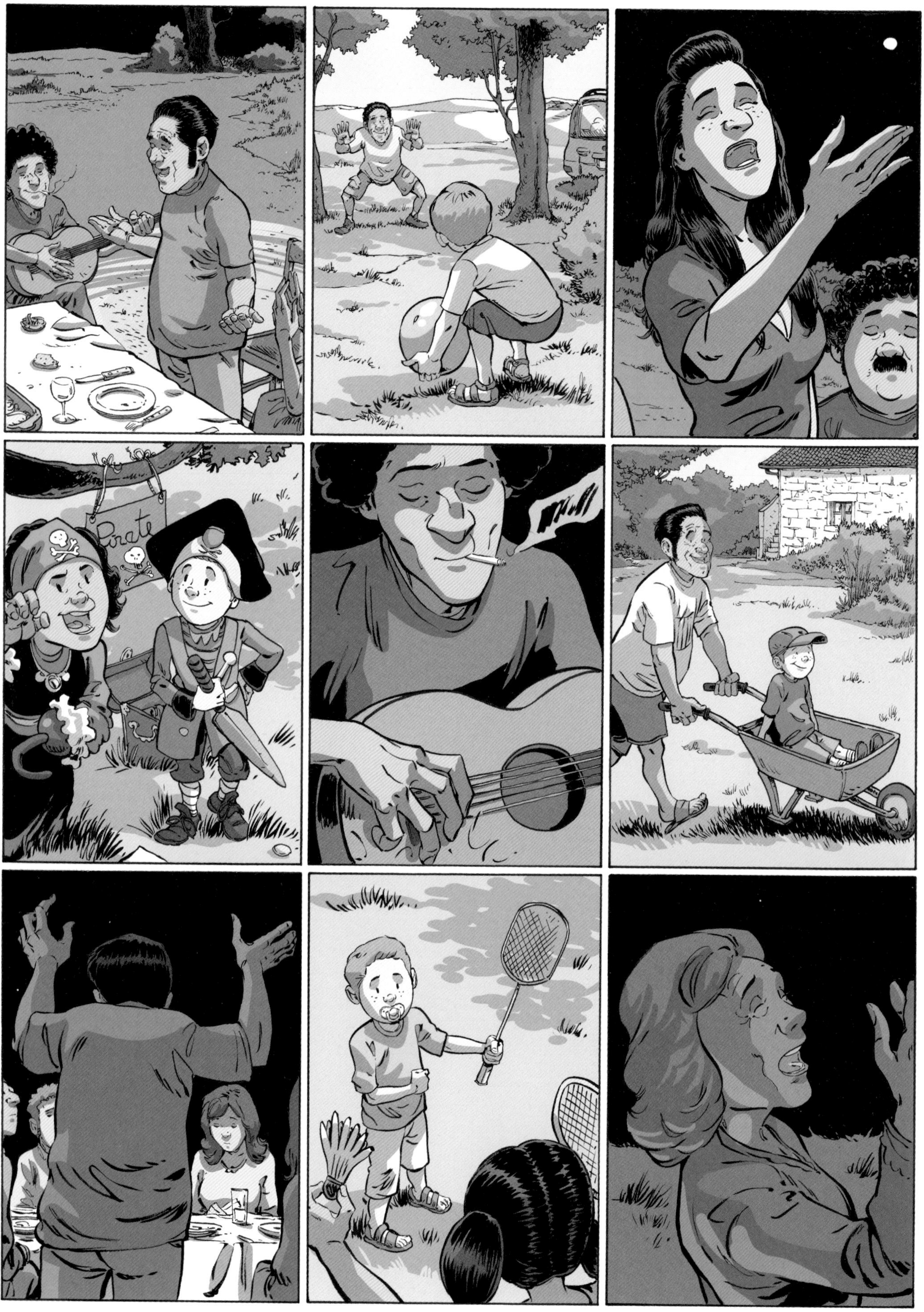
Pirate

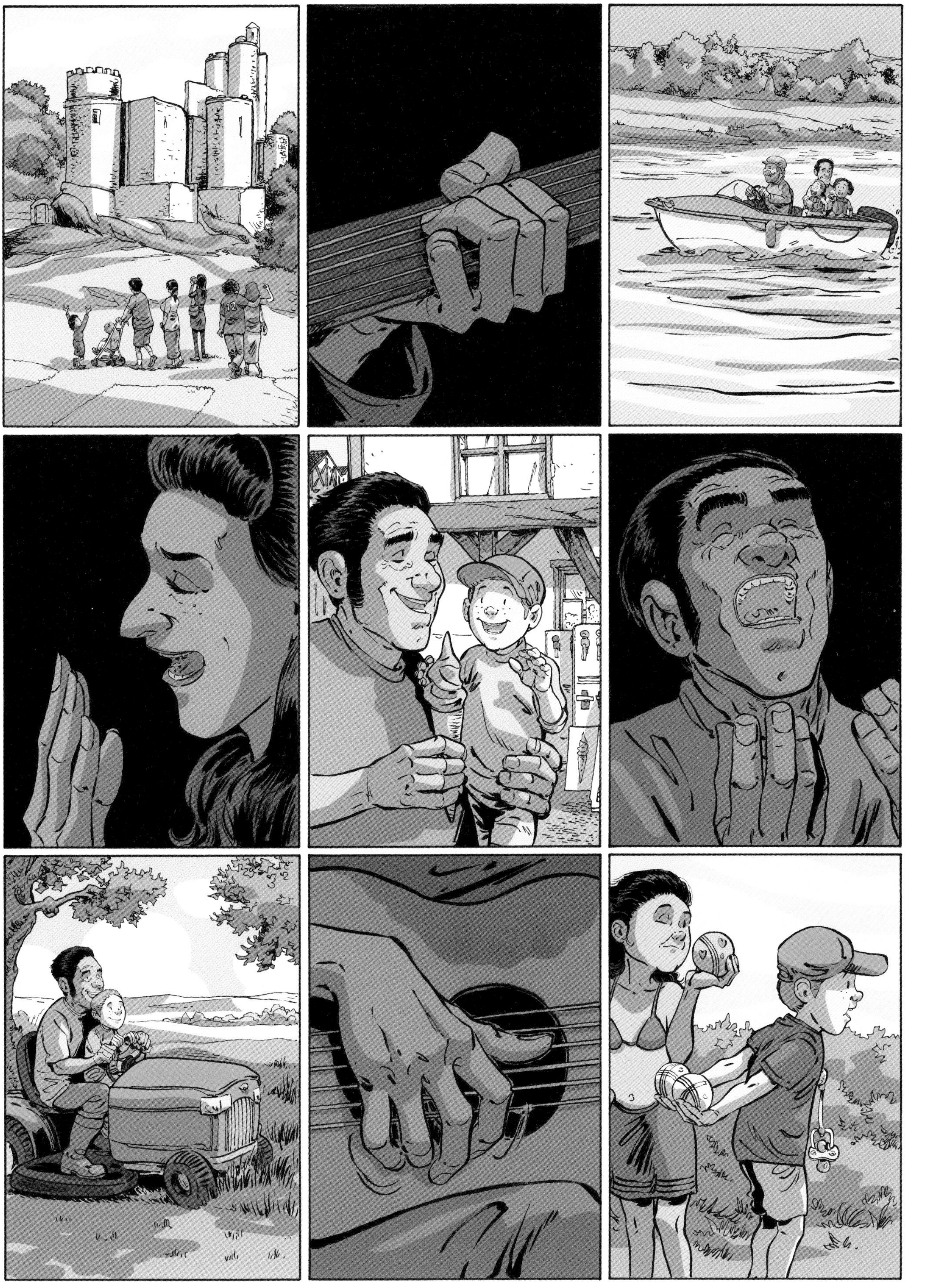

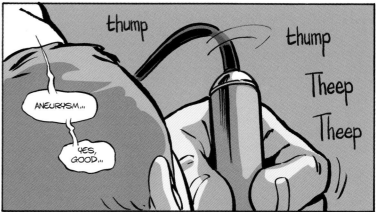

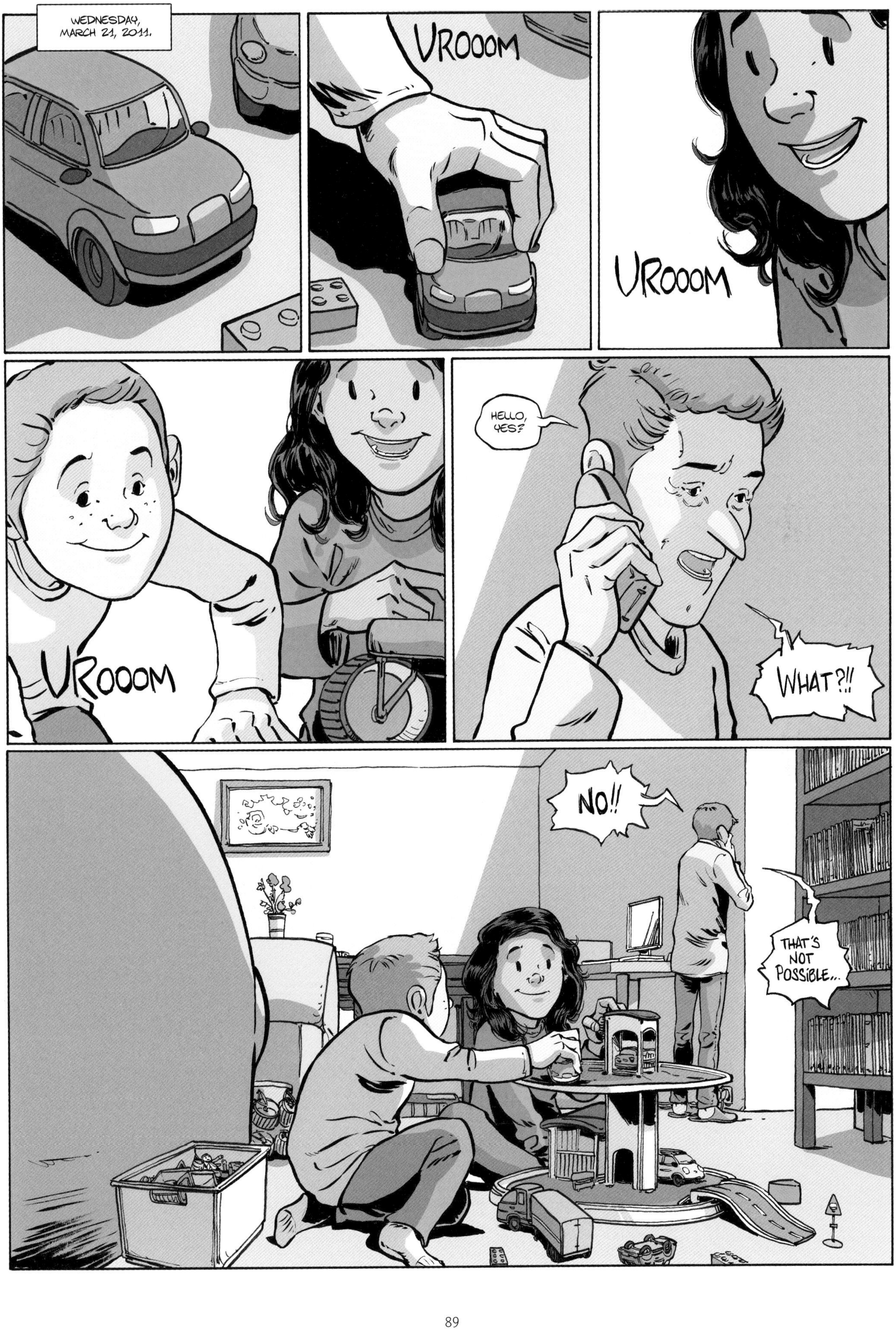
WEDNESDAY, MARCH 21, 2011.
VROOOM
VROOOM
VROOOM
HELLO, YES?
WHAT?!!
NO!!
THAT'S NOT POSSIBLE...

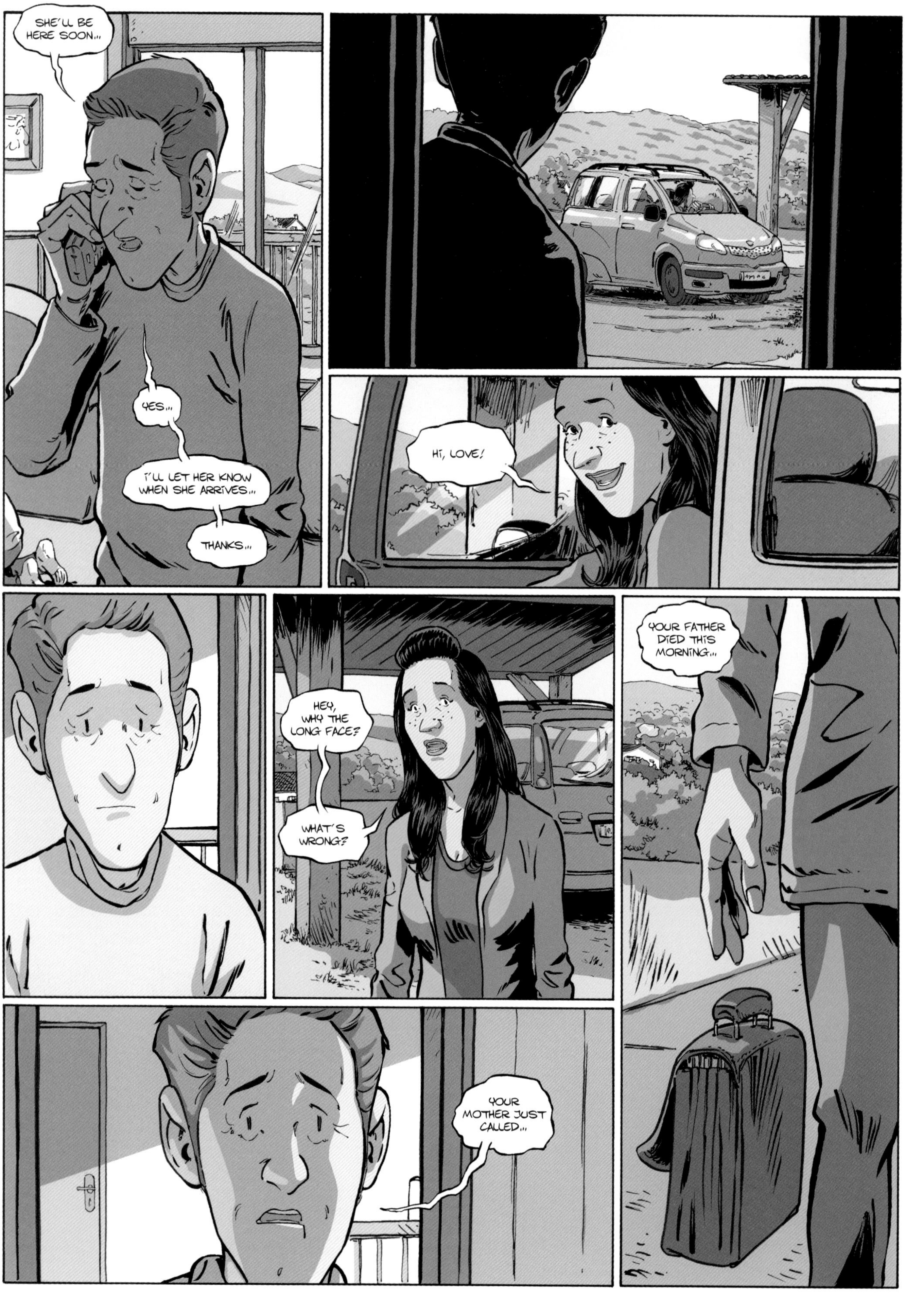
SHE'LL BE HERE SOON...
YES...
I'LL LET HER KNOW WHEN SHE ARRIVES...
THANKS...
HI, LOVE!
HEY, WHY THE LONG FACE?
WHAT'S WRONG?
YOUR FATHER DIED THIS MORNING...
YOUR MOTHER JUST CALLED...

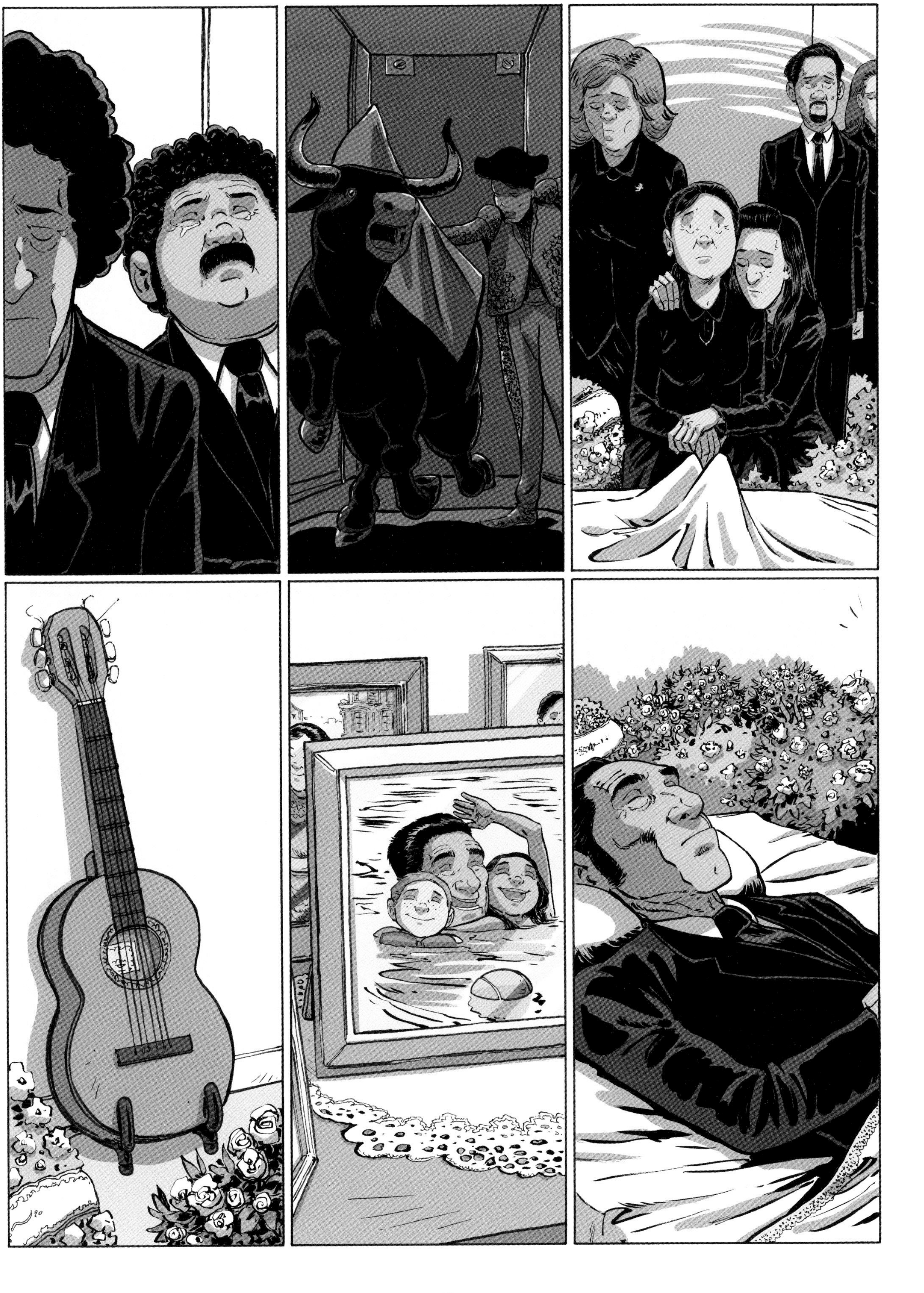

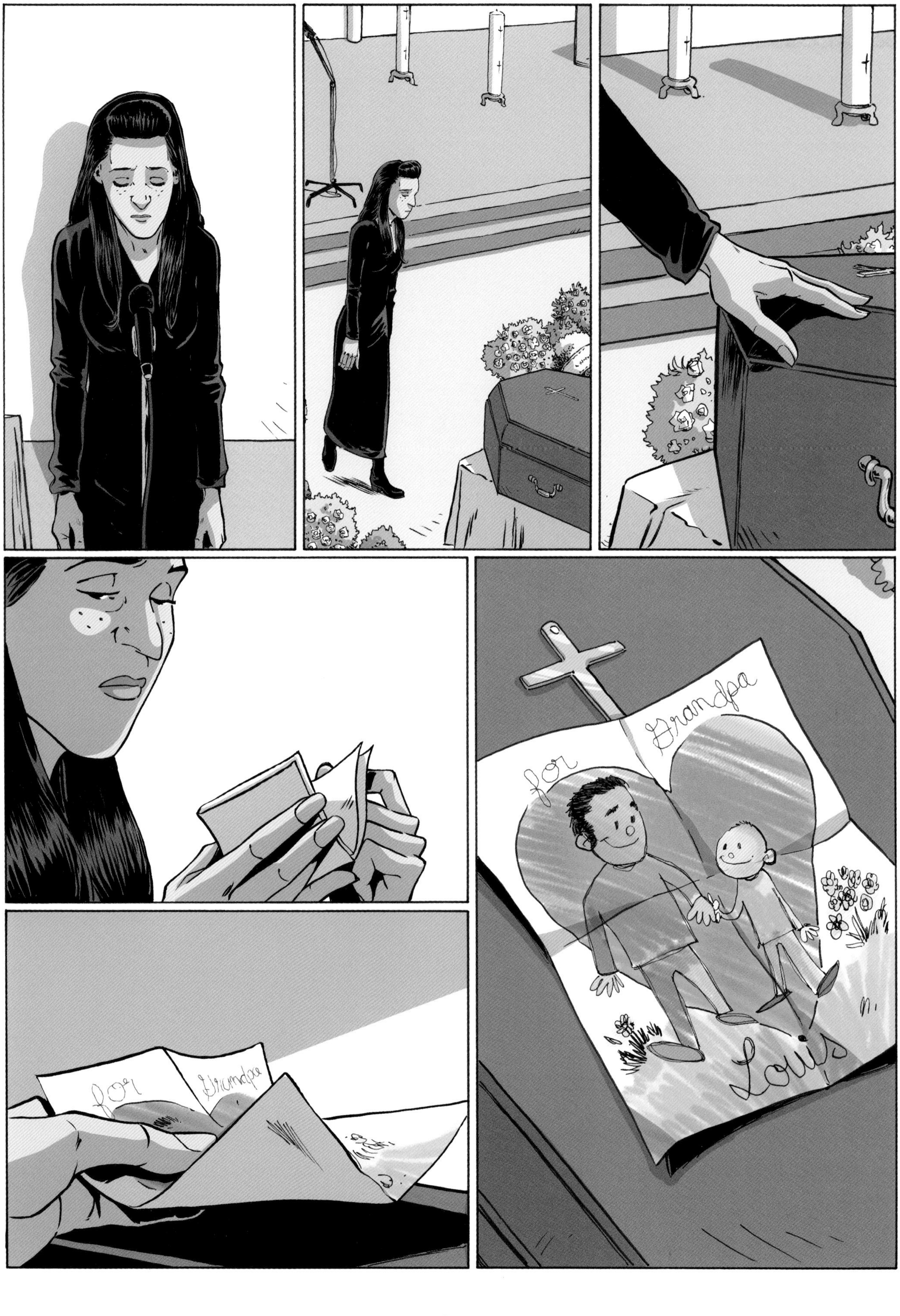
for Grandpa
Louis

EPILOGUE

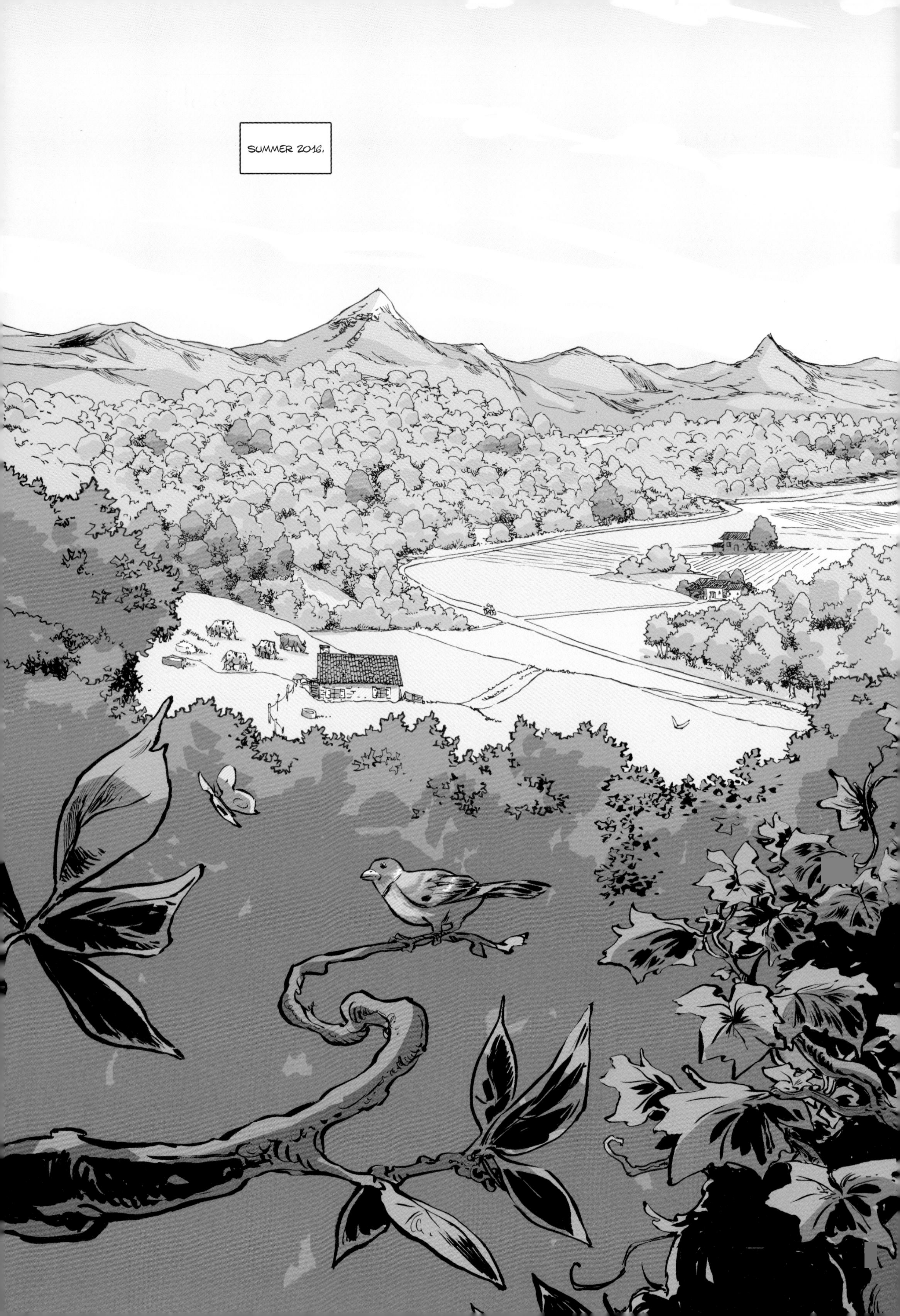
SUMMER 2016.

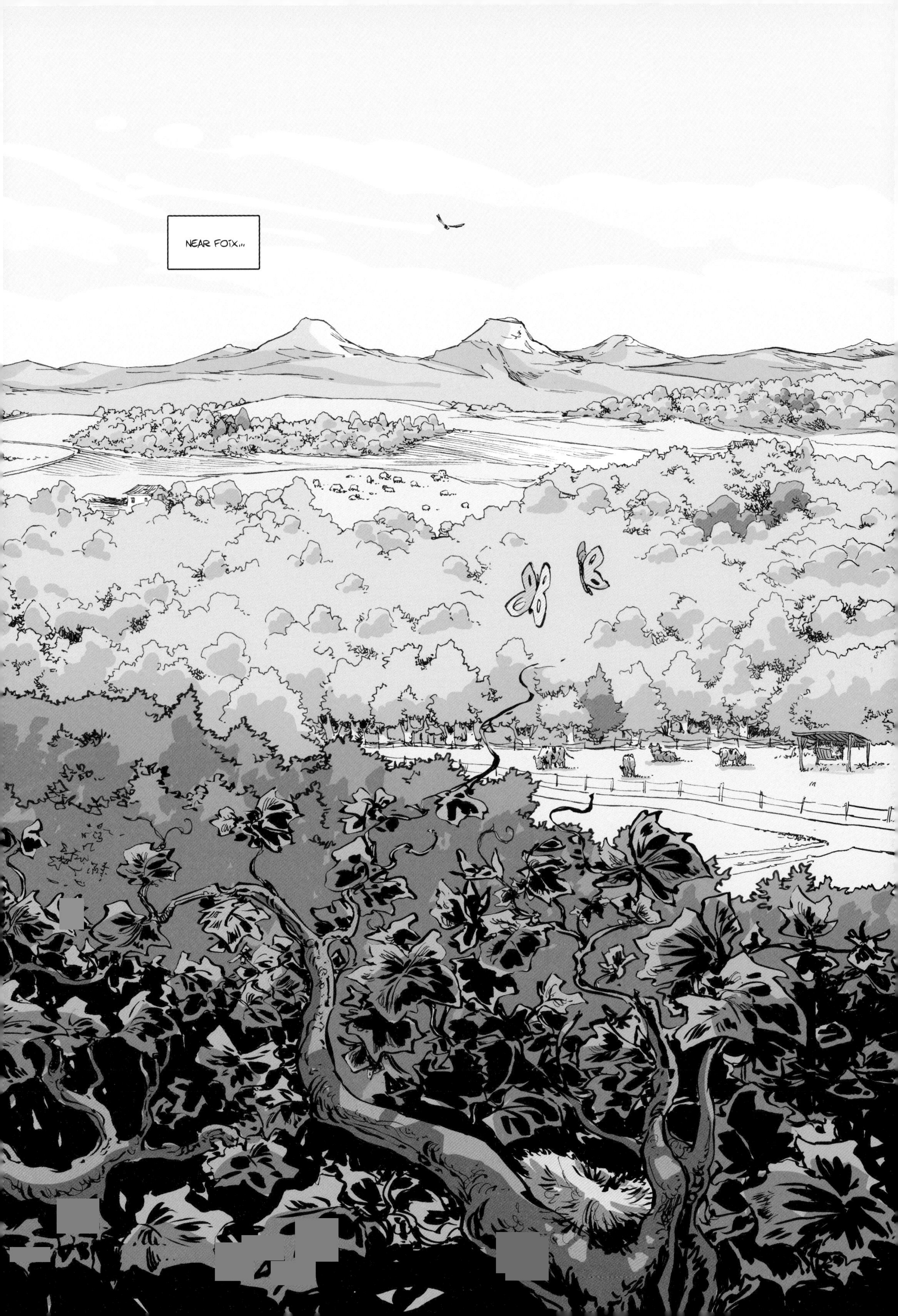
NEAR FOIX...

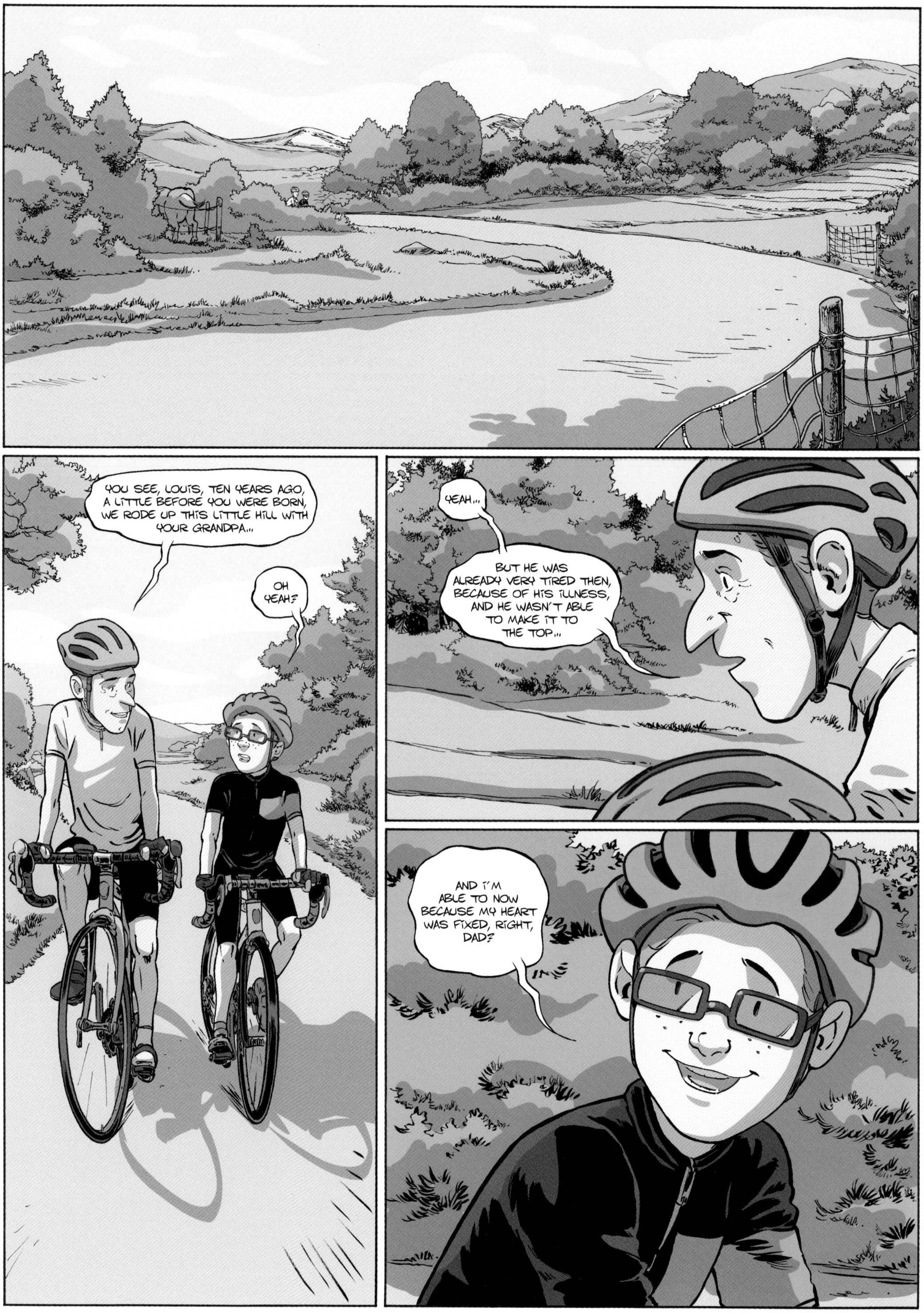
YOU SEE, LOUIS, TEN YEARS AGO, A LITTLE BEFORE YOU WERE BORN, WE RODE UP THIS LITTLE HILL WITH YOUR GRANDPA...
OH YEAH?
YEAH...
BUT HE WAS ALREADY VERY TIRED THEN, BECAUSE OF HIS ILLNESS, AND HE WASN'T ABLE TO MAKE IT TO THE TOP...
AND I'M ABLE TO NOW BECAUSE MY HEART WAS FIXED, RIGHT, DAD?

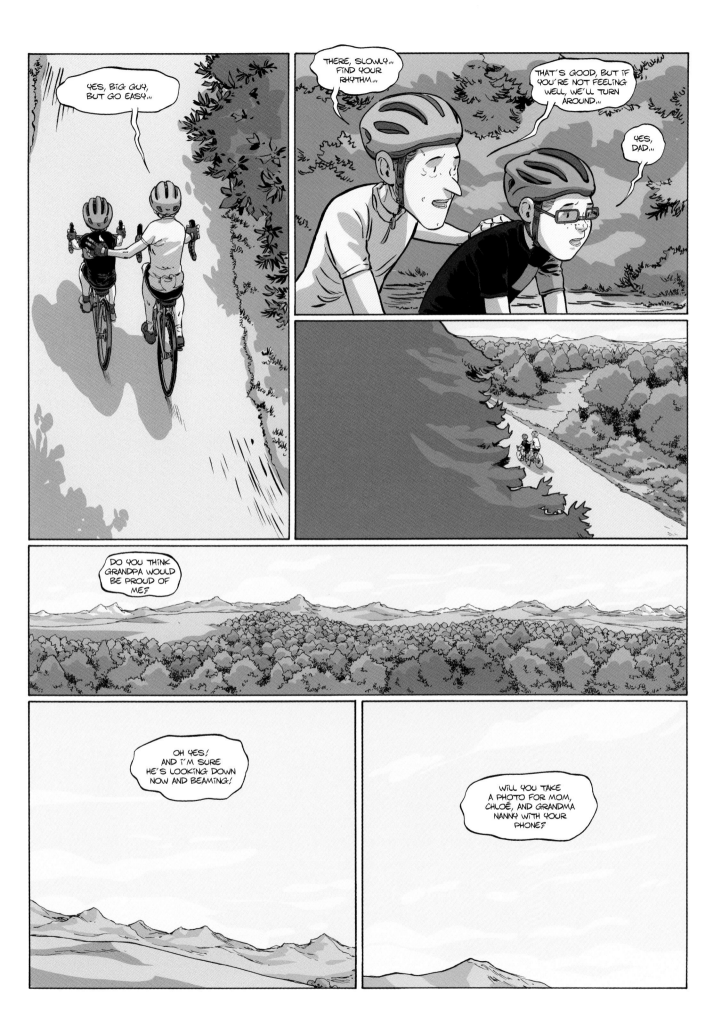

Library of Congress Cataloging-in-Publication Data

Names: Espé, author, illustrator. | Battistutta, Aretha, 1985– colorist.
Title: The pass : some stories are invented, others are told... /
writing & illustrations, Espé ; colors, Aretha Battistutta.
Other titles: Col de Py. English
Description: University Park, Pennsylvania : Graphic Mundi, [2022] |
Translation of: Le col de Py.
Summary: "A graphic novel exploring the challenges and fears of parents whose child has
been diagnosed with severe heart defects"—Provided by publisher.
Identifiers: LCCN 2021056589 | ISBN 9781637790236 (hardback)
Subjects: LCSH: Pediatric cardiology—Comic books, strips, etc. | Heart—Abnormalities—
Comic books, strips, etc. | Children—Surgery—Comic books, strips, etc. | Heart—Abnormali-
ties—Surgery—Comic books, strips, etc. | Parent and child—Psychological aspects—Comic
books, strips, etc. | LCGFT: Graphic novels.
Classification: LCC PN6747.E87 C6513 2022 | DDC 741.5/944—dc23/eng/20220104
LC record available at https://lccn.loc.gov/2021056589

Printed in Lithuania by BALTO Print
Published by The Pennsylvania State University Press,
University Park, PA 16802–1003

Graphic Mundi is an imprint of The Pennsylvania State University Press.

Translated by J.T. Mahany

Le Col de Py © Bamboo Edition, Espé

The Pennsylvania State University Press is a member
of the Association of University Presses.

It is the policy of The Pennsylvania State University Press to use acid-free paper.
Publications on uncoated stock satisfy the minimum requirements of
American National Standard for Information Sciences—Permanence of Paper for
Printed Library Material, ANSI Z39.48–1992.